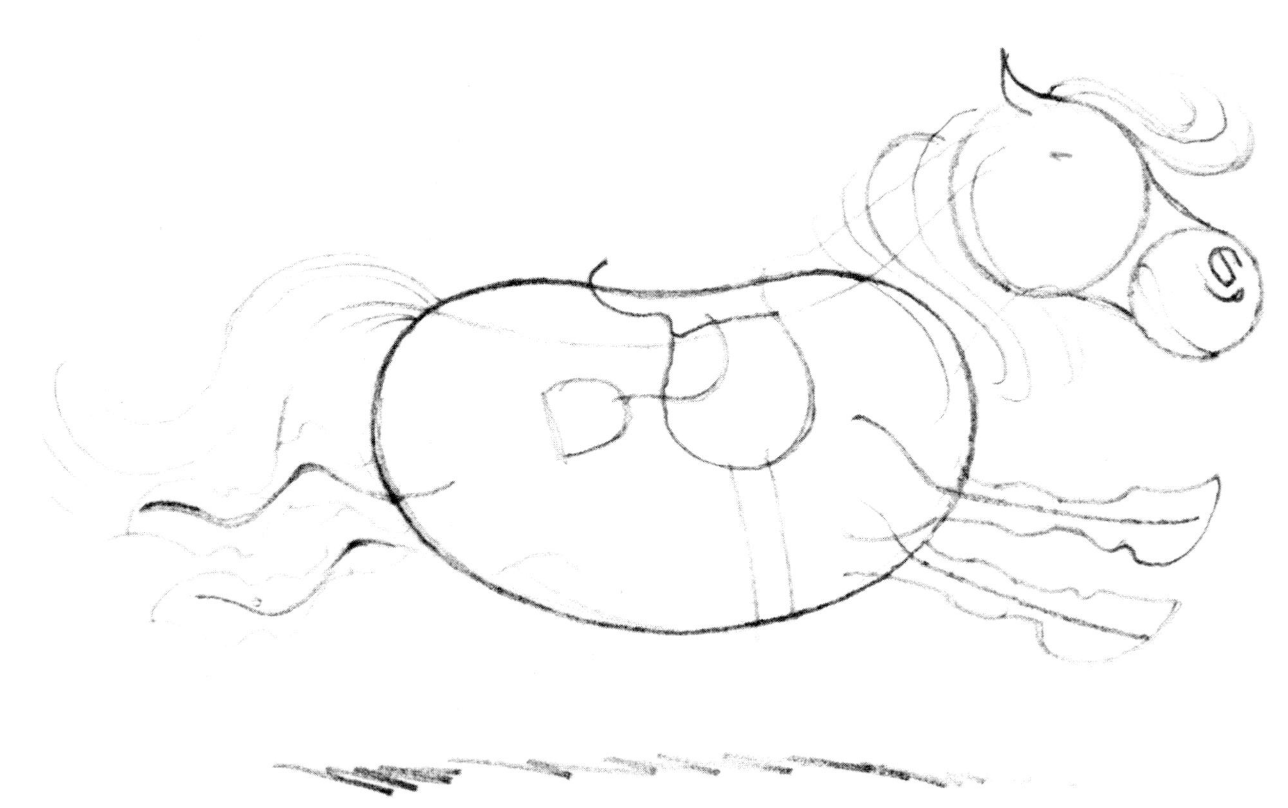

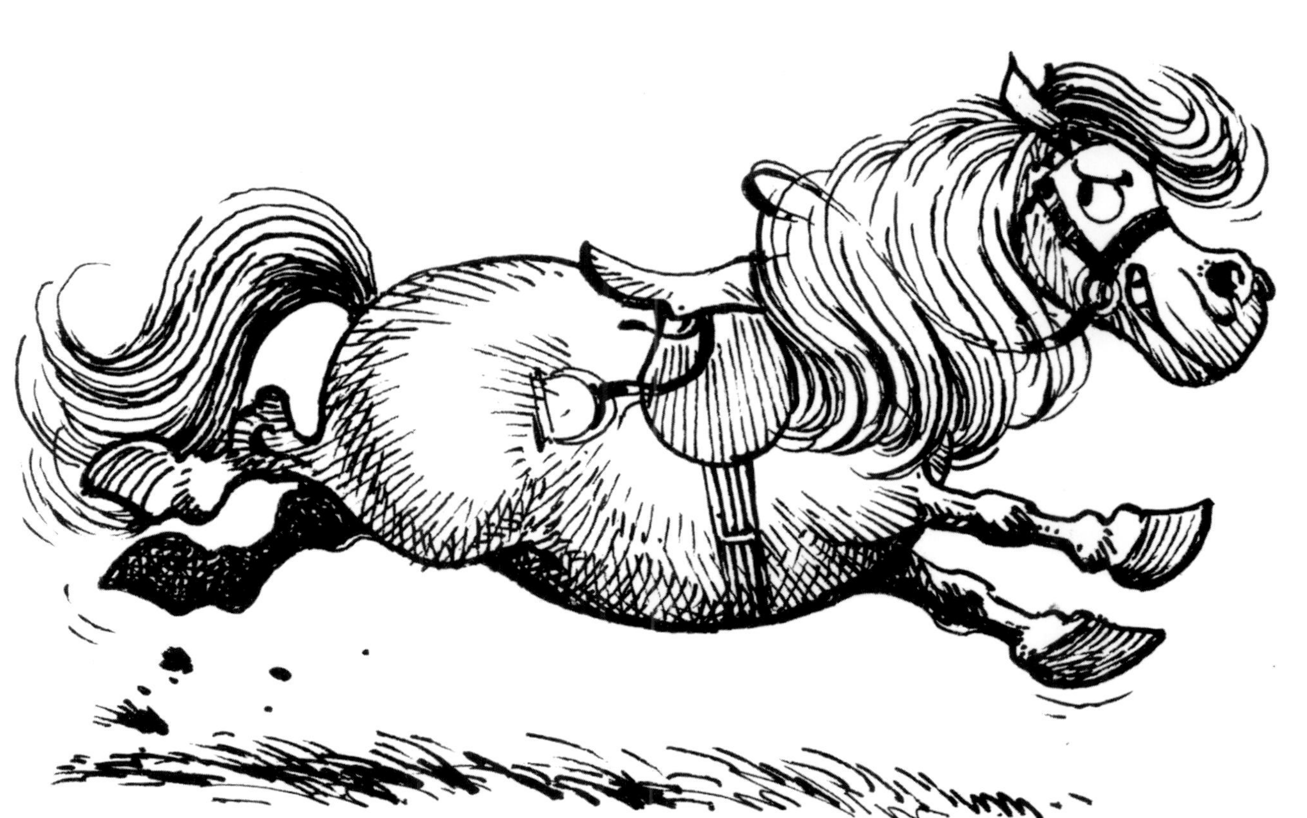

In 1952, Norman Thelwell (1923–2004) penned his first cartoon for the satirical British magazine *Punch*, renowned internationally for its wit, irreverence, and for publishing the world's best comic writers and poets. This led to a relationship that lasted for 25 years and over 1,000 cartoons, including 60 front covers. Thelwell was a master of sharp social comment and humour, and his 34 books have sold millions of copies worldwide and have been translated into numerous languages (www.thelwell.org.uk).

Also by Norman Thelwell and published by Quiller
The Effluent Society
Some Damn Fool's Signed the Rubens Again

HOW TO DRAW PONIES

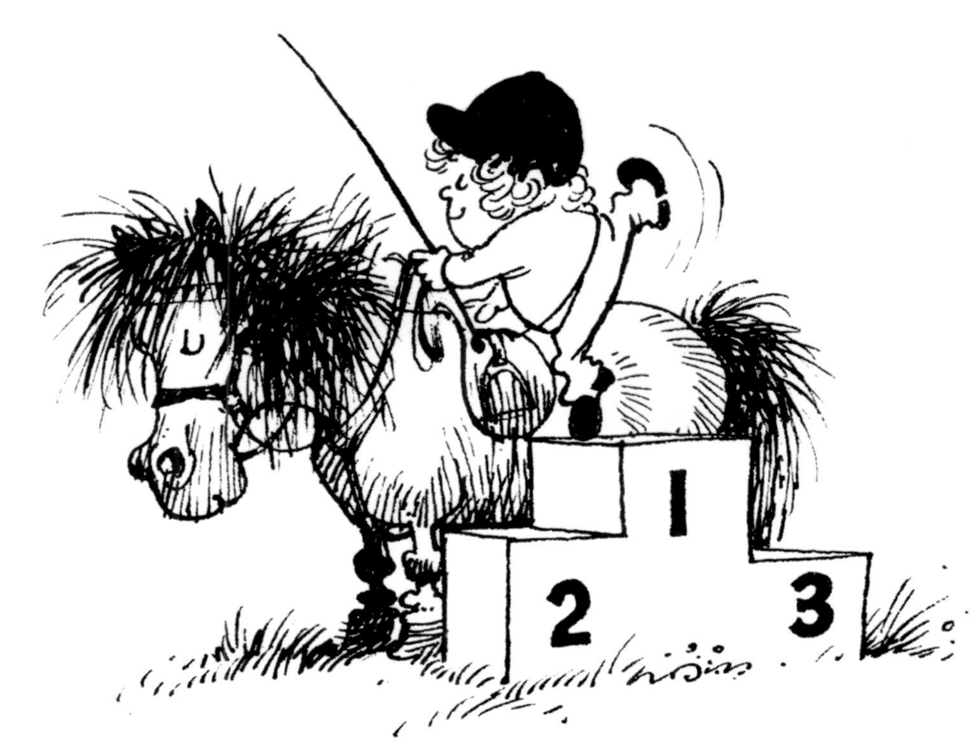

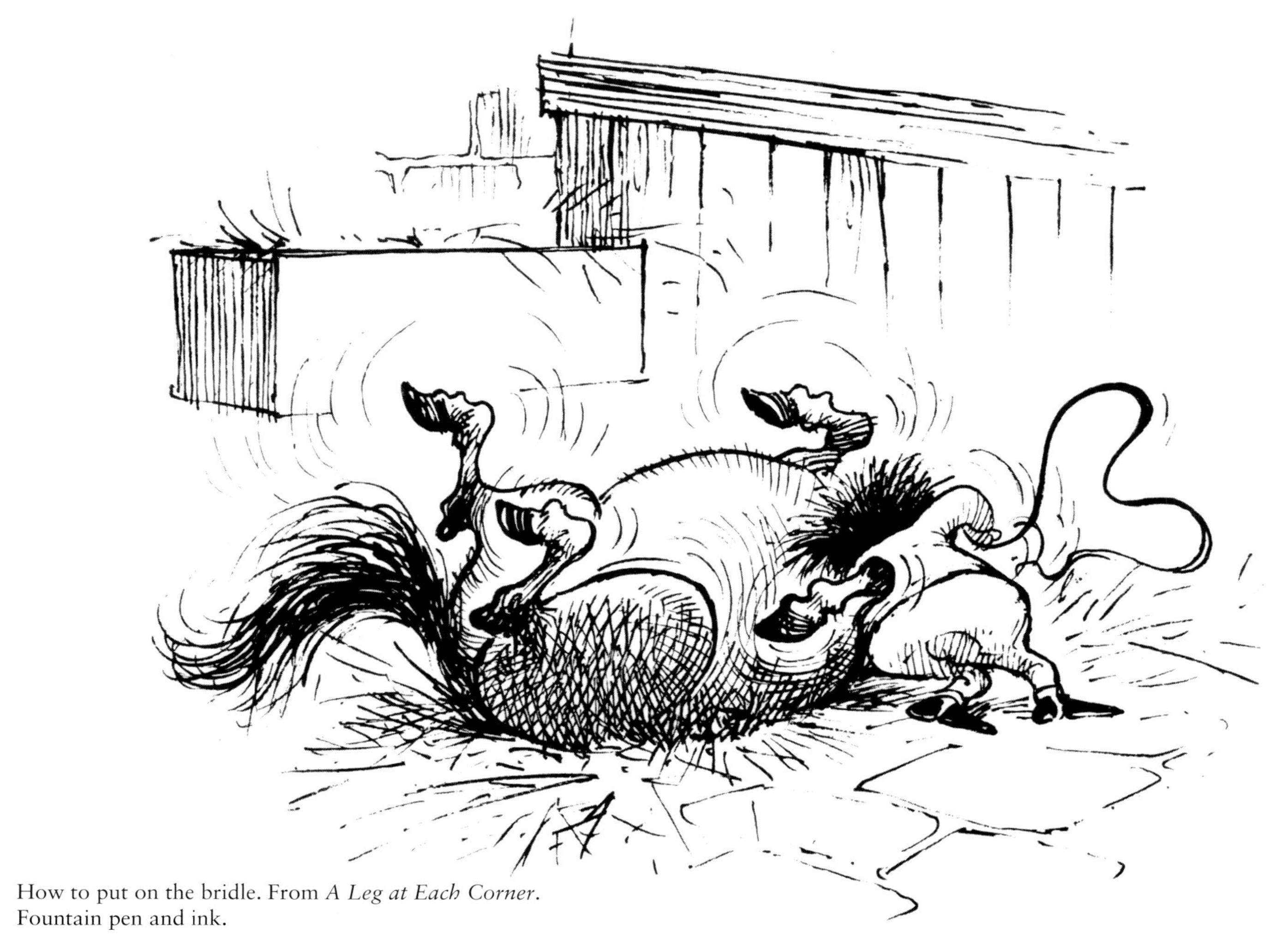

How to put on the bridle. From *A Leg at Each Corner*.
Fountain pen and ink.

HOW TO DRAW PONIES

ALL THE SECRETS REVEALED BY

thelwell.

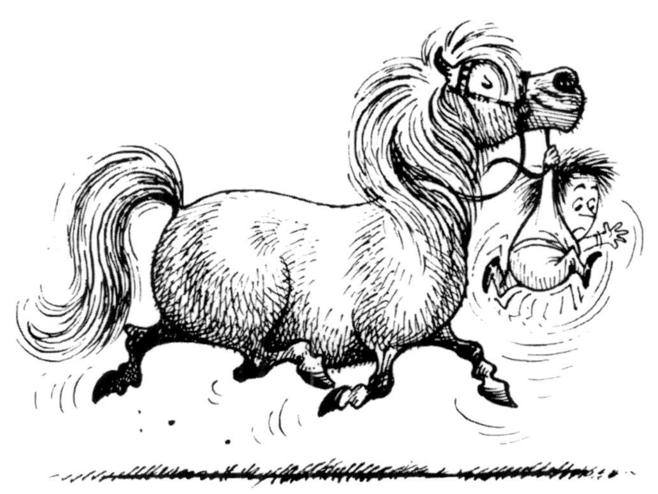

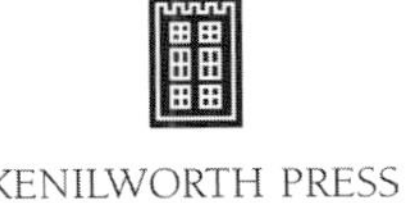

KENILWORTH PRESS

First published in 1982 by Methuen London Ltd

This edition published in the UK in 2025 by
Kenilworth Press
An imprint of Quiller Publishing
The Hill, Stroud
Gloucestershire, GL5 4EP

www.quillerpublishing.com

ISBN 978-1-910016-60-2 (hardback)
ISBN 978-1-910016-61-9 (ebook)

British Library Cataloguing in Publication Data.
A catalogue record for this book is available from the British
Library.

1 2 3 4 5 6 7 8 9 10

Typesetting by SJmagic DESIGN SERVICES, India.
Printed in the UK.

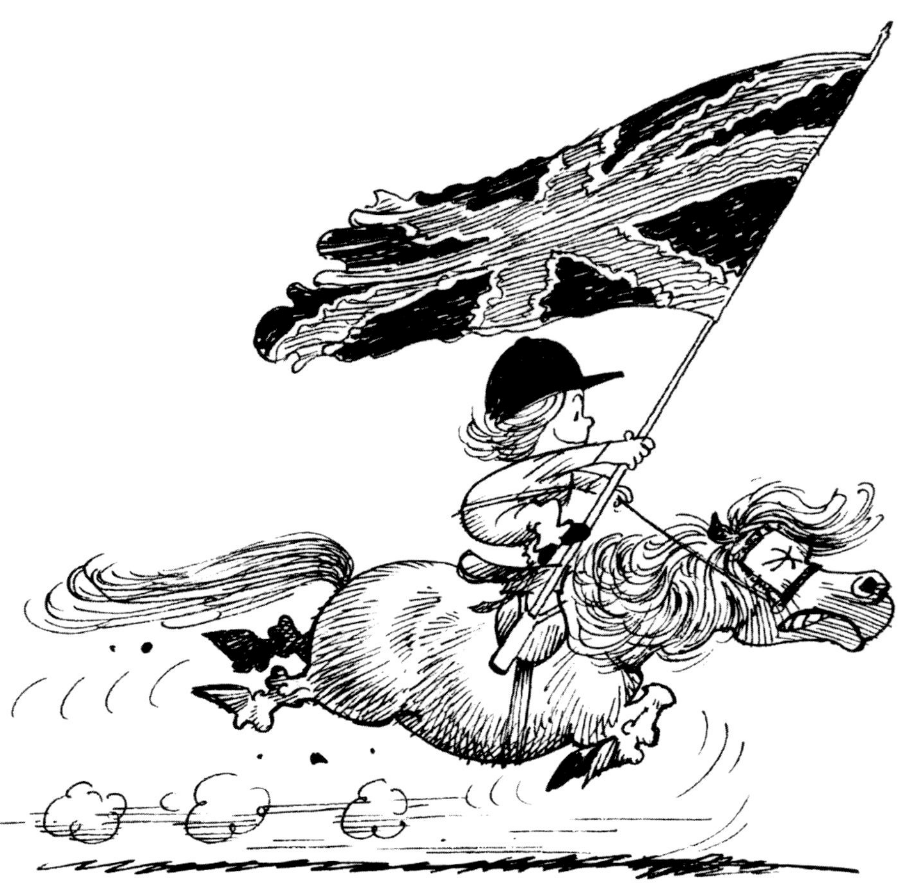

Contents

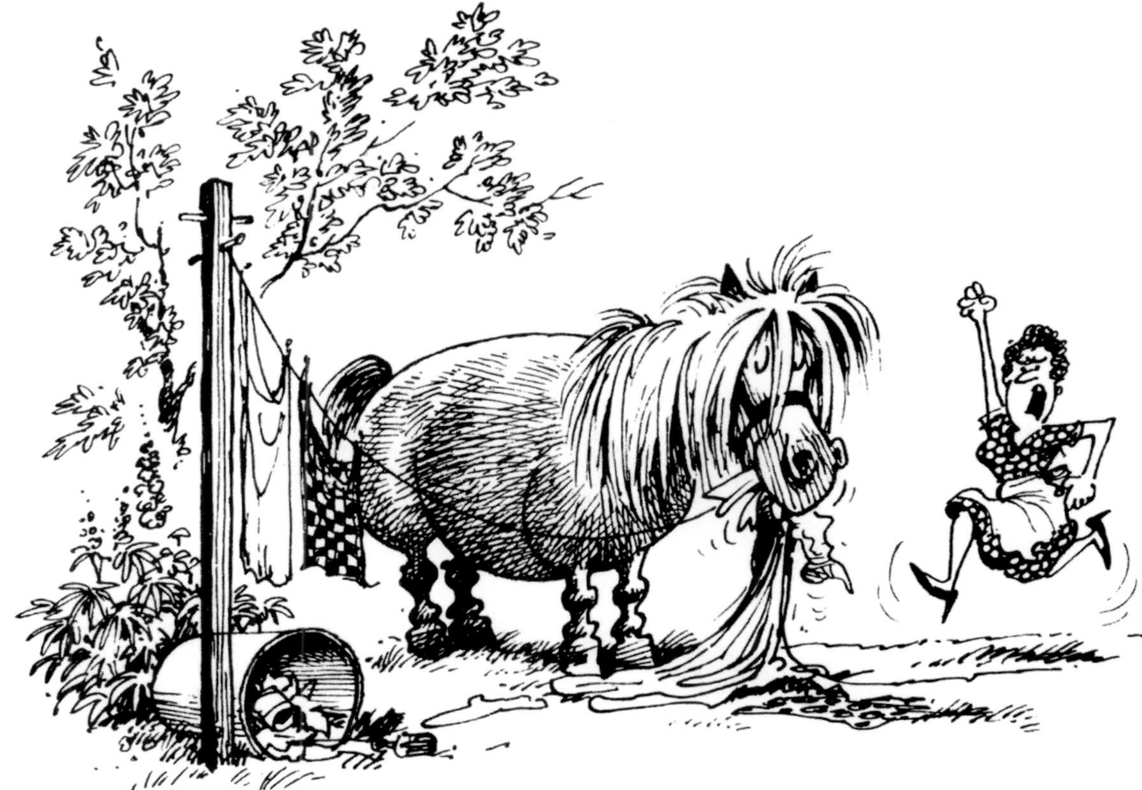

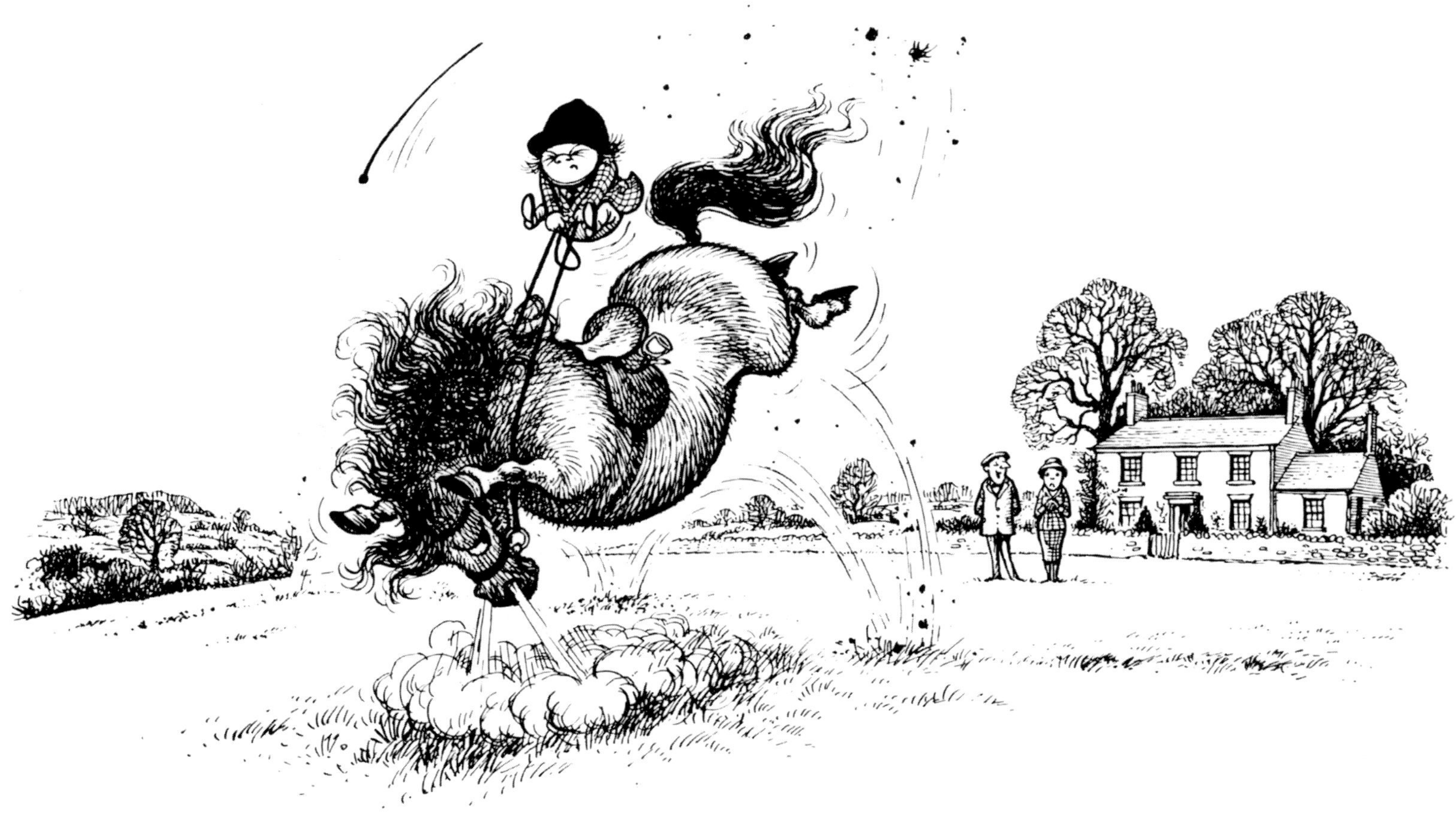

'That's *one* Christmas present she won't break in a hurry.'

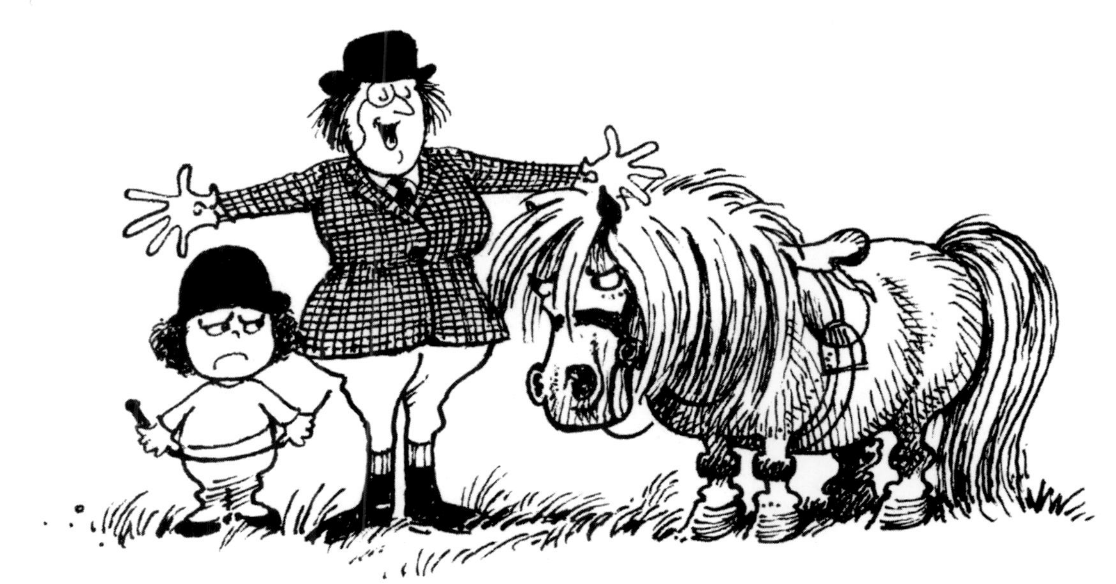

Introduction

In the course of my work as an illustrator and cartoonist, I have drawn almost every subject under the sun at one time or another, or so it seems to me: human beings, animals, machinery, landscape and architecture, roller coasters and rockets, parrots, planets and pigs. I have been asked many questions too, such as 'Where do you get your ideas?' and 'Do you get paid for your drawings?' But the most frequent question is 'How do you draw those ponies?'

Why ponies should be singled out in this way I am not sure, and the simple, truthful answer 'The same way that I draw anything else' does not seem to satisfy anyone.

It is not easy to answer this question more fully on a street corner, or on the telephone, or even in a letter. I'm not all that sure that I shall find it easy in a book either, but I am going to try.

There are no short cuts to drawing well, just as there are no short cuts to doing anything worthwhile, but it is interesting to know how other people go about their work, and sometimes it is helpful. I hope that these pages may be helpful to you.

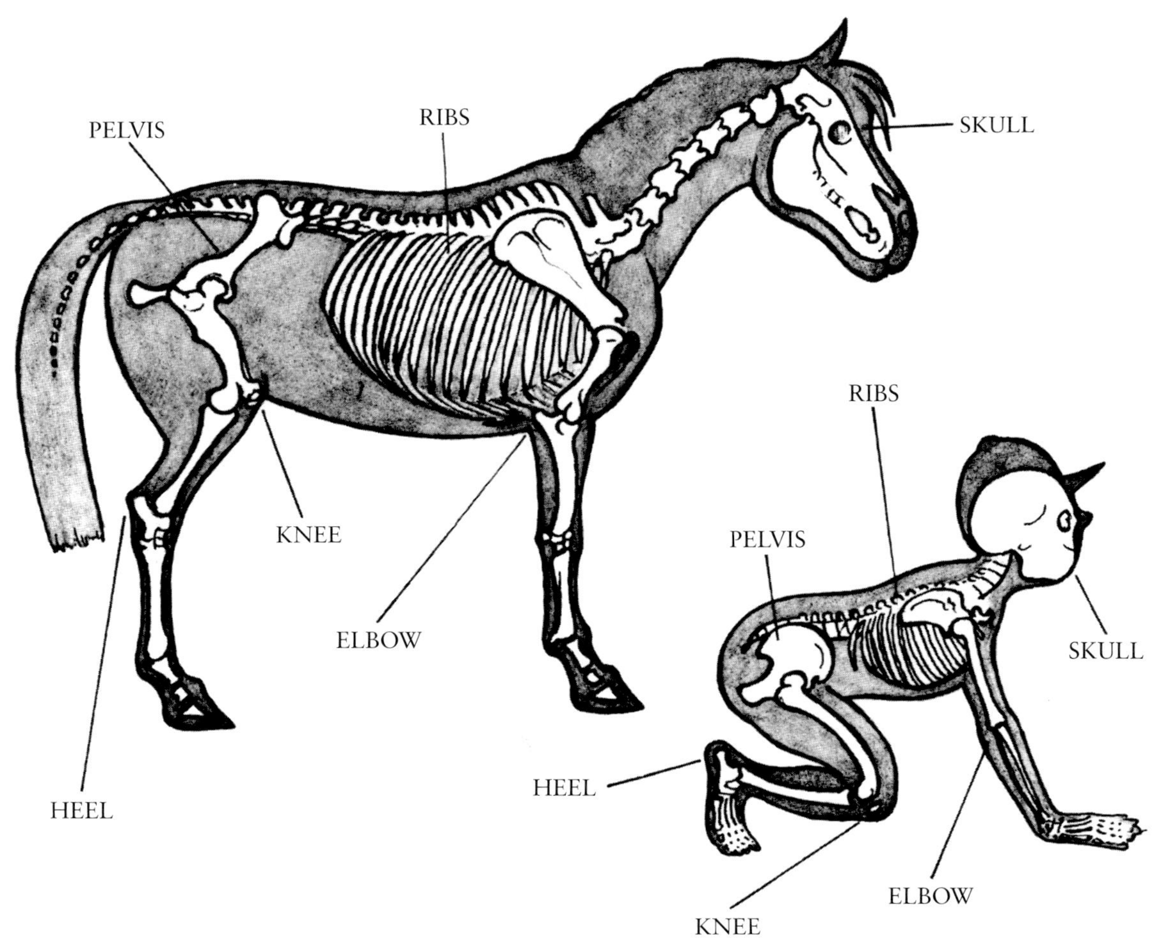

PELVIS
RIBS
SKULL
KNEE
ELBOW
HEEL
RIBS
PELVIS
SKULL
HEEL
ELBOW
KNEE

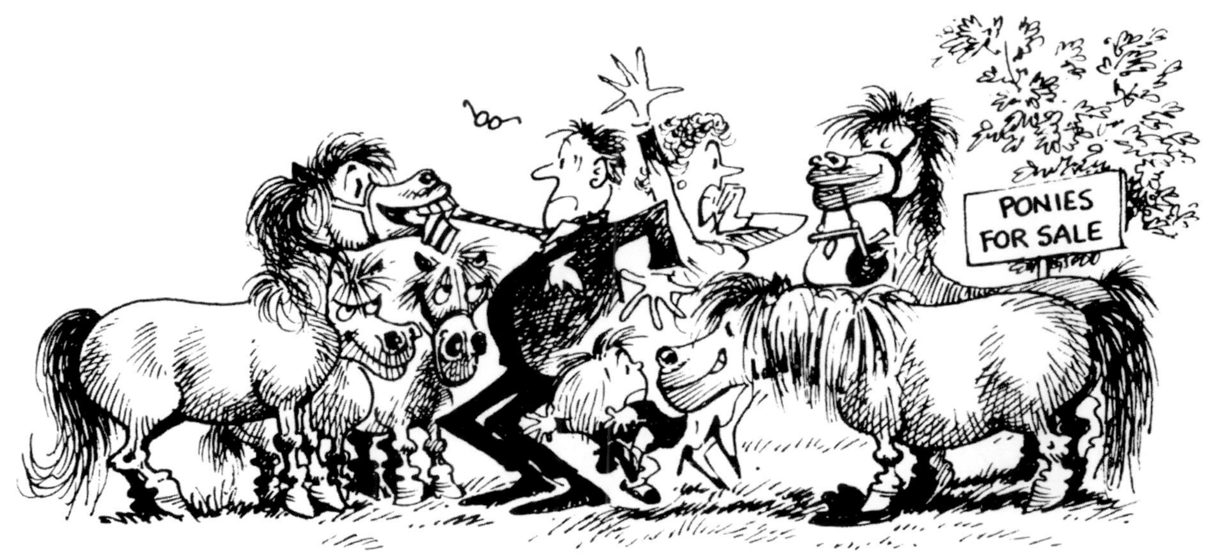

What is a pony?

Well, it may surprise you to know that in many ways he is very like a human being. Look at the diagram on the opposite page. You will see that he has a skull, a rib cage and a pelvic bone, and so have we. These are all joined together by his spine in much the same way as ours.

He has an extended spine which forms his tail, of course, but we also have a tiny tail which does not show on the outside.

Let us think of our arms as front (or fore) legs. His fore legs are connected to his rib cage by flat sheets of muscle which hold his shoulder blades in place. His hind legs fit into hollows in his pelvis, making a smooth ball and socket joint. This is true of us too.

At first glance his hind legs look very different from our own, but they are really very similar. His thigh bone is shorter in proportion, but it is otherwise much the same, and although his knee is high and close in to his body, it is constructed much like ours and works in a similar way.

EAR
POLL
FORE LOCK
BROW
MANE
WITHERS
CHEEK
THROAT
TAIL
CROUP
LOINS
BACK
NECK
HAUNCH
SHOULDER
BUTTOCK
RIBS
STIFLE
FLANK
ELBOW
BREAST
ABDOMEN
HOCK
FORE ARM
KNEE
CANNON BONE
PASTERN
FETLOCK
CORONET
HOOF

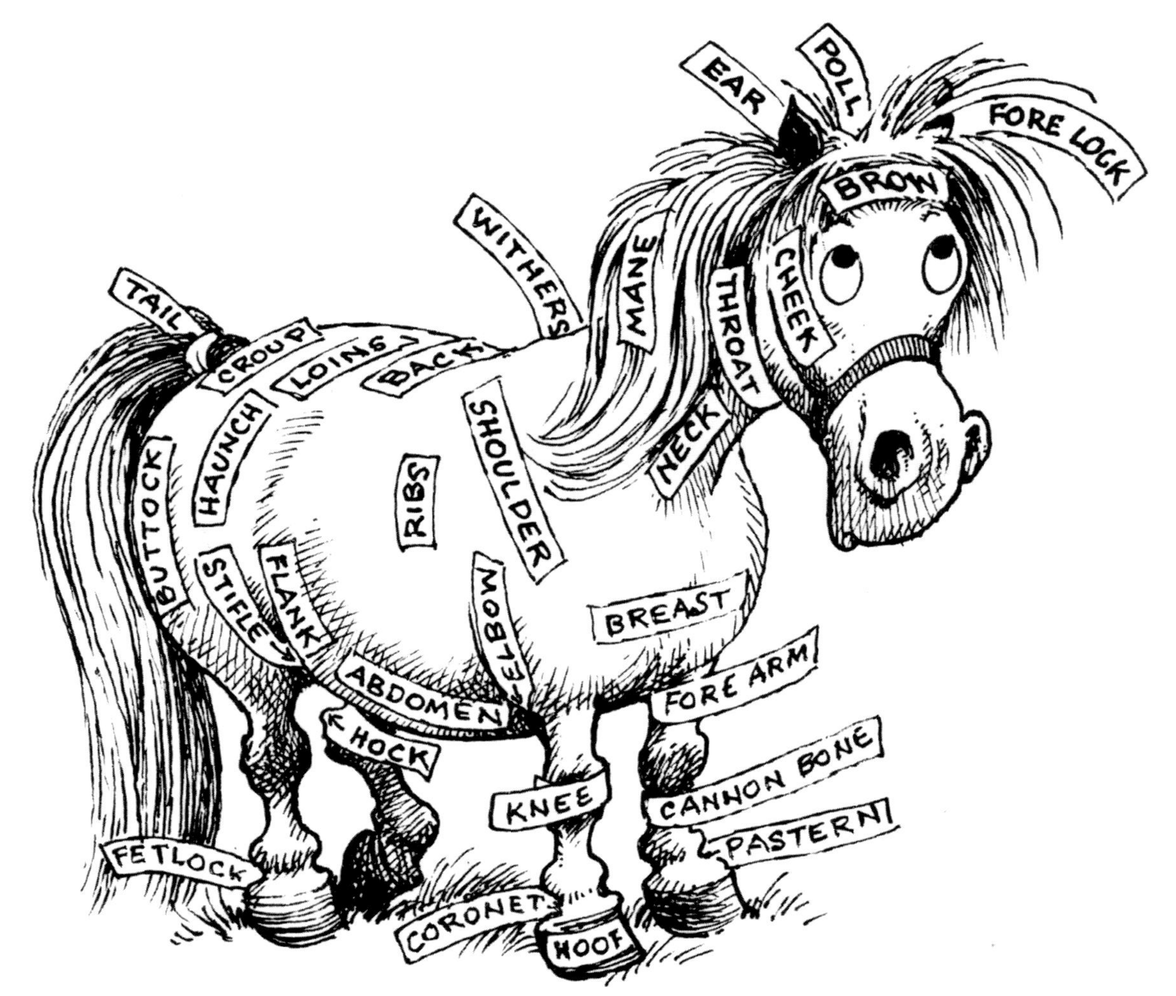

14

We have a shin bone below the knee, and our heel and toe bones are connected to this. A pony also has a similar bone below his knee to which his heel and toe bones are attached. It is important, when thinking about how ponies move, to remember that this joint is really his heel. Now a rather interesting thing happens; we have five sets of toe bones, all rather short and each with a nail at the end. A pony has disposed of all but the centre toe, and this has become very big and strong, and his toe nail has become very useful indeed for walking on and for kicking other people's ponies.

If we now look at our 'fore' legs, the story is much the same. We both have shoulder blades which slide smoothly against our rib cages. A pony has an upper arm bone like us, but shorter and thicker and held in against his side so that his elbow joint is tucked in close to his chest. Our lower arm has two bones, his only one; at the point we often wrongly think of as his knee, he has no knee cap but a series of little bones very like those in our wrist.

It is odd to think that if we put our pony wrongly at a jump, he is likely to fall on his wrist. But this is so, and it explains why this joint is so easily damaged by a bad fall. If it were really his knee, then he would have a knee cap to protect it.

The fore legs of a pony finish off in a similar way to his hind legs, but he has developed a strong finger at the front to match the strong toe at the back.

So there you are. Whether we like it or not, we are all a bit horsey.

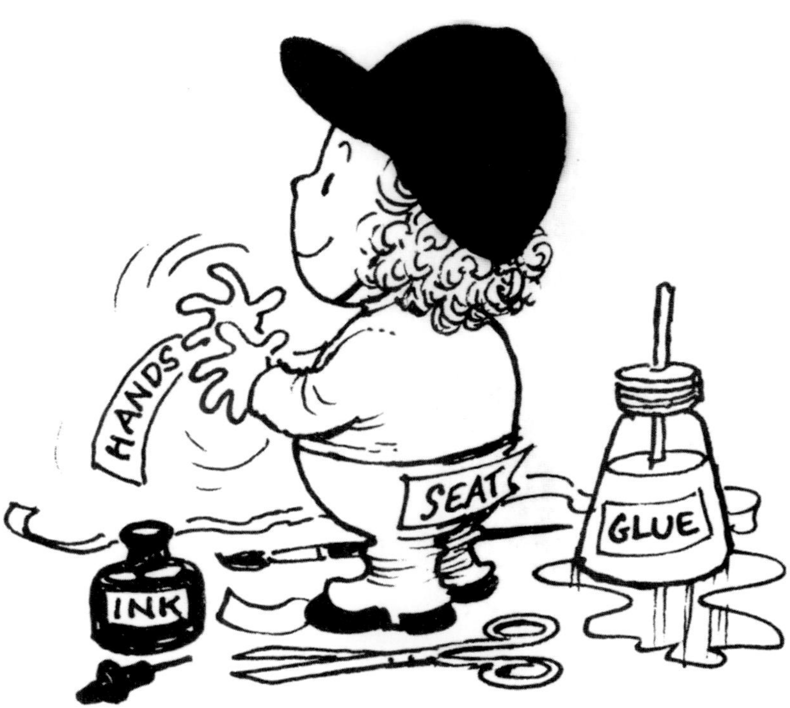

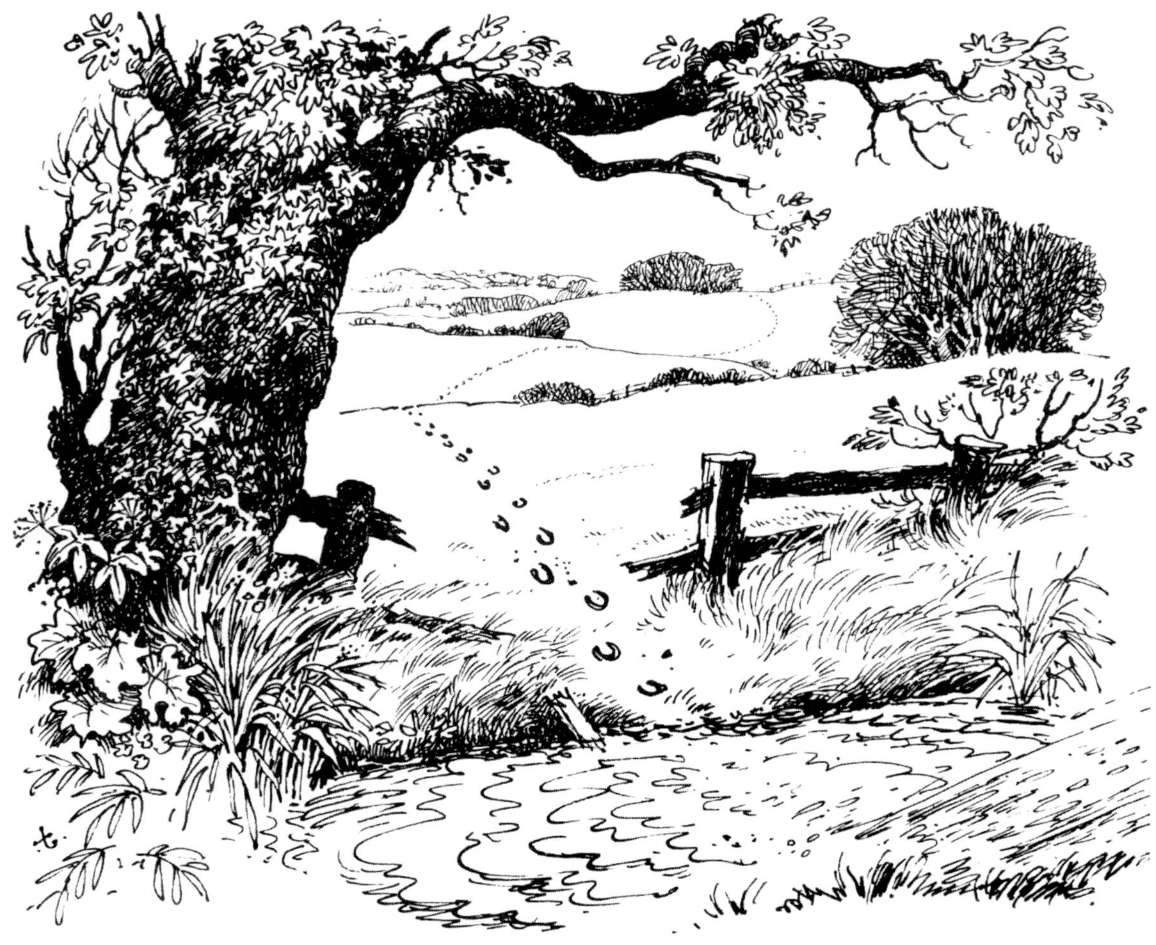

Feeling like a pony

This comparison of the structure of a pony and of ourselves is not only interesting but very important if we wish to draw ponies. We can only express ourselves well in graphic form if we have a real feeling for our subject.

To draw a pony convincingly we must identify ourselves with him. We must walk, trot, canter and gallop as he does, at least in our minds, and try to understand what it feels like to be put at a high fence when we don't want to jump. Then perhaps we will get our expressions right when we knock it down and fall on our wrists.

We must show his feelings in our drawings mainly by facial expression, but remember that his face is very different from ours, at least as far as most of us are concerned. When we give him expressions which are really human ones, we must be very careful indeed not to destroy his character as an animal.

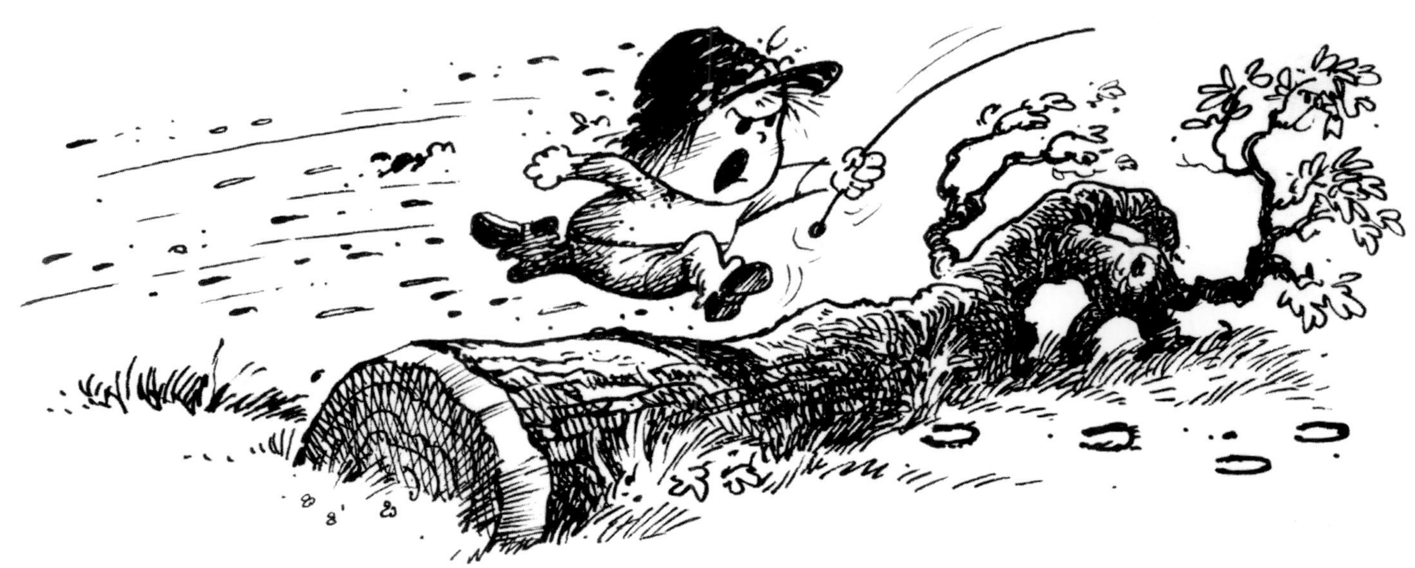

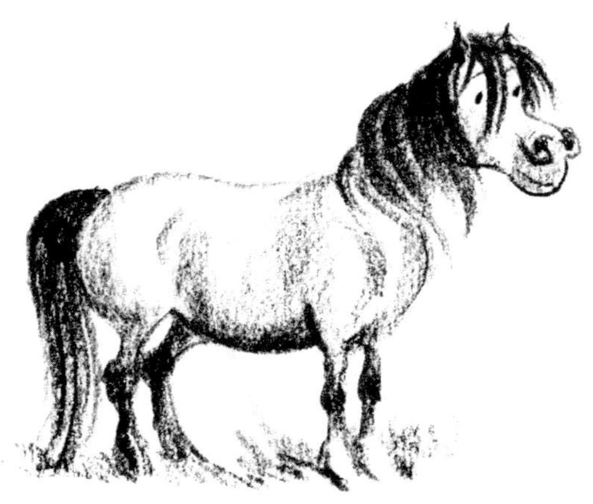

Lithographic crayon

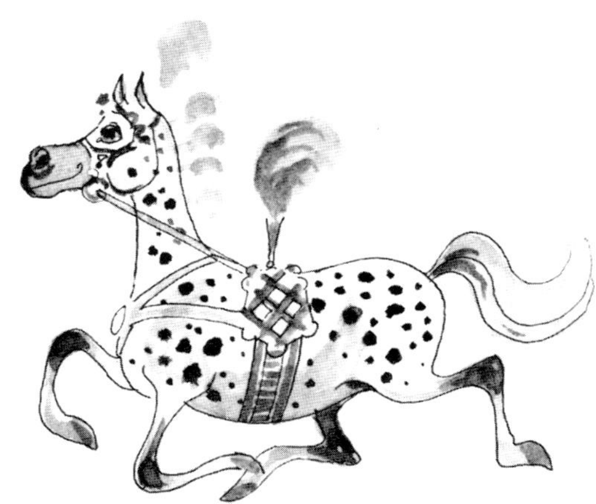

Line and wash

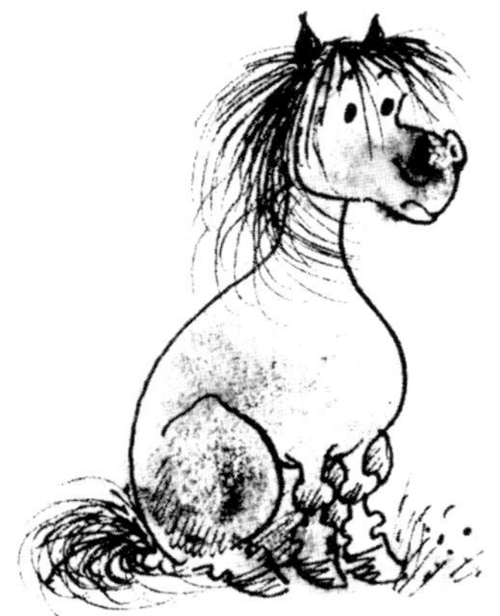

Unfixed fountain pen ink and wet thumb

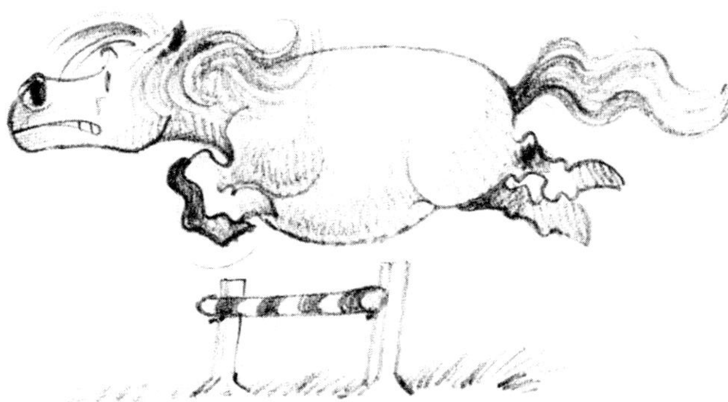

Pencil

Materials

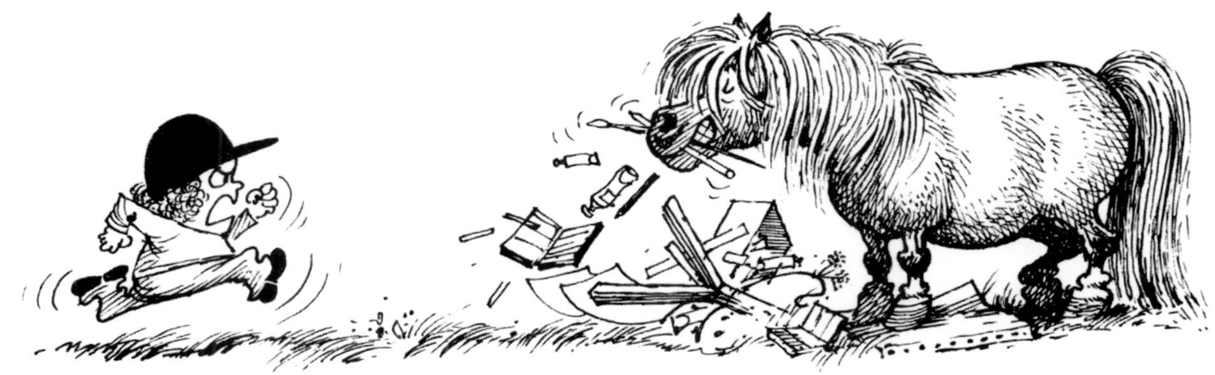

As with most things about drawing and painting, there are no strict rules about materials unless you are drawing for a magazine, book or newspaper. If you are, then you must make it your business to find out from the editor what materials you are allowed to use. If you use the wrong ones, it may not be possible to reproduce your work in that particular publication and the editor will not be pleased.

Most drawings are done in black Indian ink with a pen, or sometimes a brush, on a good quality white paper or fashion board. This sort of work is clear and easy to print, and Indian ink is very black and does not smudge. I do not use Indian ink if I can avoid it, because it tends to thicken quickly in the bottle and on the nib when you are drawing, and this can be a great nuisance. I also dislike bottles of ink because they are so easily knocked over and they tend to distract one from the job in hand.

A fountain pen is an ideal drawing instrument, if you can find one which gives you a wide variety of line and will run smoothly on the paper. There are a number of makes of black fountain pen ink which will give a good black line and not clog the pen as Indian ink would certainly do.

It must be remembered, however, that fountain pen ink will smudge if roughly handled, and some editors do not like it.

If you are drawing purely for pleasure, then you should try any materials that you can get hold of. You will soon discover those that suit you best, and you will have no end of fun trying different paper surfaces with inks, chalks, crayons, pens and paints.

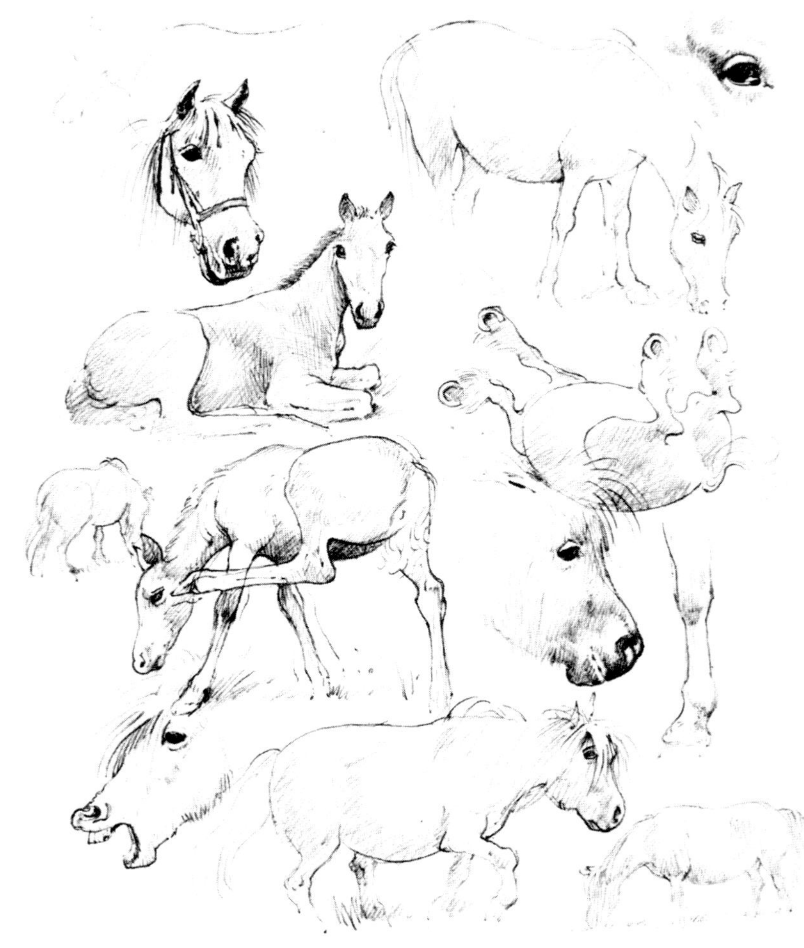

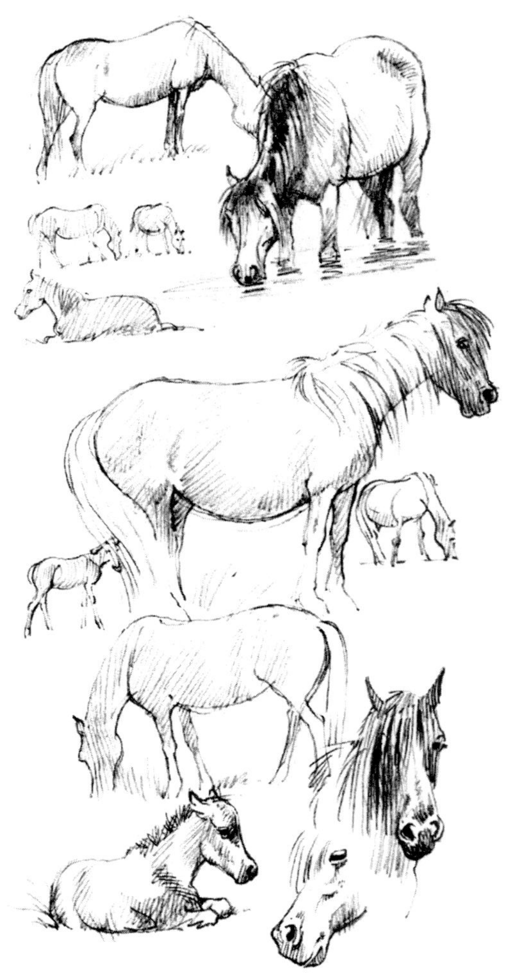

A closer look

We have seen that in some respects a pony is not unlike ourselves.

In many ways, however, he is very different, and if we are to make him look convincing on paper we must find out more about him.

This we must do with the aid of a sketchbook, the most valuable piece of an artist's equipment. Take one with you wherever you go, and draw in it as much and as often as you can.

Draw horses and ponies at shows, grazing in fields and standing in stables; anywhere and everywhere that you can find them.

If they are moving, then make a lot of quick sketches on the same sheet, going from one sketch to another and back again as the animal changes position.

The best way to learn how to draw is by drawing, and by doing it as often as possible. Do this with ponies and horses and you will learn a great deal and improve your draughtsmanship at the same time.

Getting down to work

Although it is most important to draw from life whenever possible, to improve both one's drawing ability and one's knowledge of horses, there is of course no question of using models directly when creating one's own personal equine world. This world is a personal one, and within it we may do whatever we choose provided that we achieve the results we are after. One's imagination and invention will influence the way one interprets nature on paper. Everyone draws differently, just as no two people use quite the same handwriting.

One's style of drawing will develop naturally from a combination of technical ability and imagination. Don't try to force yourself into a style or manner of drawing. Let it develop in its own way. It is a great help to look at other people's work and to learn from it, but it is fatal to be influenced too much by the work of one particular artist. If you copy another man's work, you can never produce more than a pale imitation.

However, you must make a start somewhere, and knowing how other people go about their work can be very helpful in setting you off on your own particular road.

Start drawing by putting down the general mass and proportion of the animal and arranging it in a convincing manner.

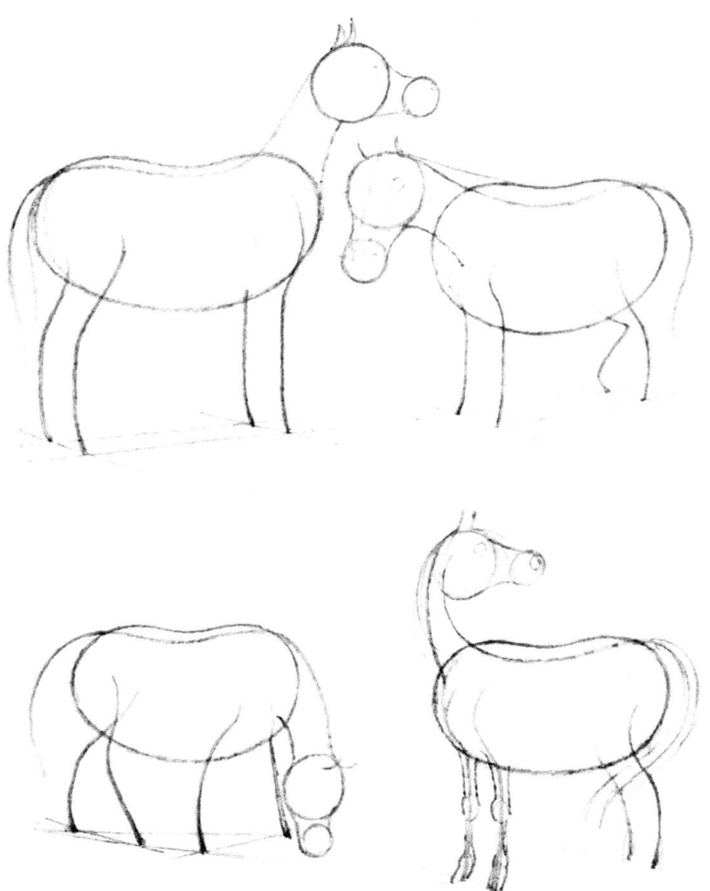

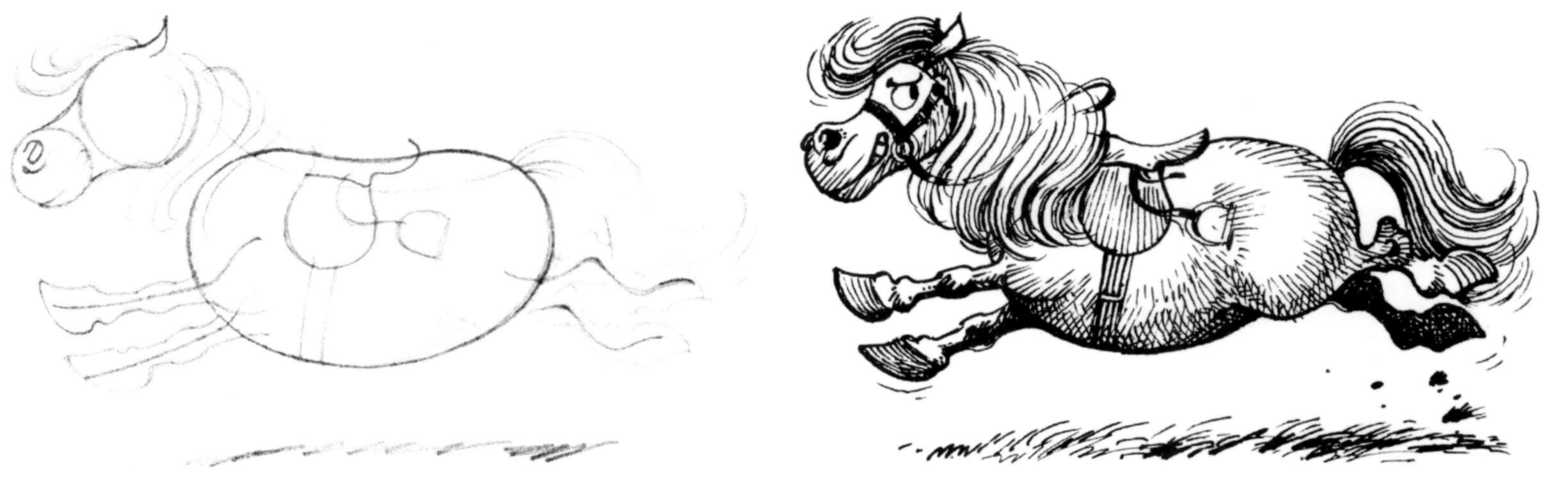

This is best done by thinking of the body as a bean or kidney shape, the head as a sphere with a smaller one beside it, and the limbs as flexible wires attached to the bean. Another and most important flexible wire joins the head to the body, passing beneath the upper surface of the bean and ending in the tail.

Thus you have a simple horse puppet which can be drawn quickly and easily. Its lack of surface detail is a great help at this stage, for you can devote your full attention to proportion and arrangement. You can play about easily with these few simple shapes until you are quite sure you have the sort of action you require and the type of animal you want, whether long and thin or short and fat.

It is at this stage also that you must think of the human beings who may be included in the drawing. The best horsemen try to ride as if they were part of the horse. Balance between horse and rider is not only essential in

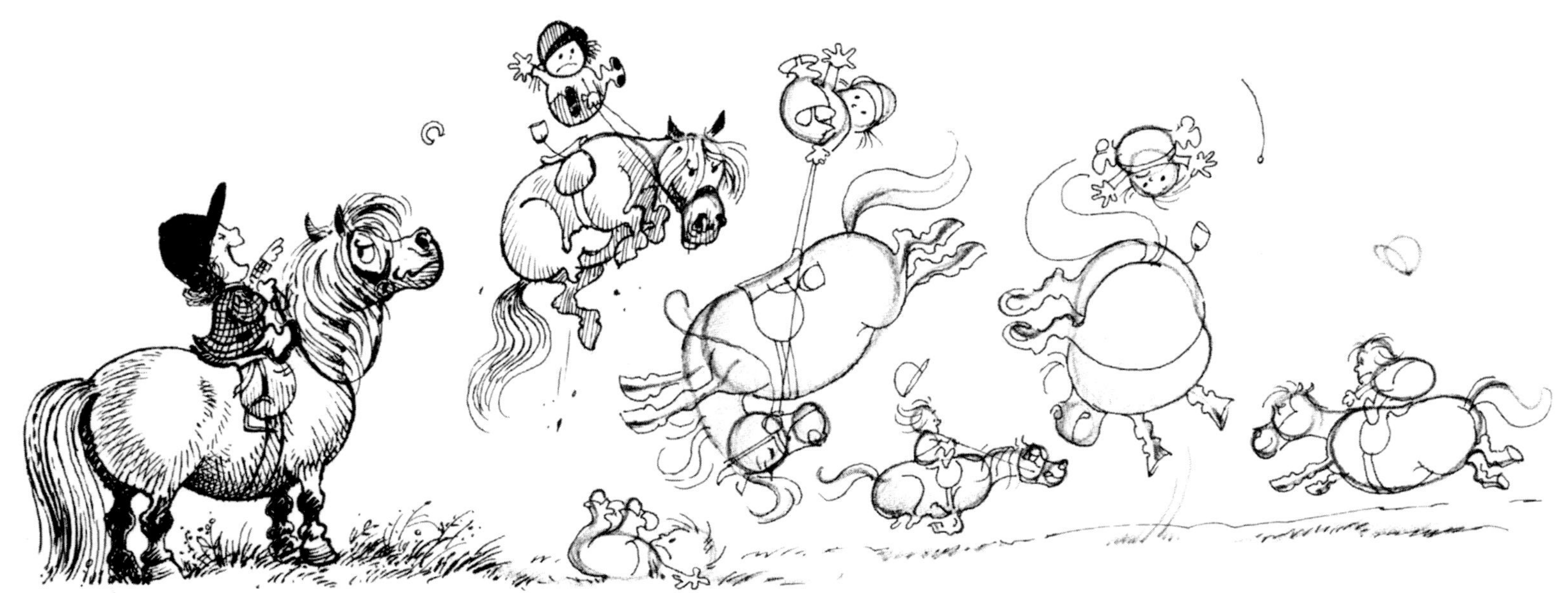

real life, it is vital also in drawings. Never think of the rider separately from the horse.

The rider must never be an afterthought to be added later if you feel like it. Horse and rider must be thought of together and drawn together right from the start.

In the same way that you can use a few basic shapes for the horse, the human figure can be represented in a simplified manner. This enables you to work out the relative proportion and position of the rider in relation to his mount right from the start.

For the human figure use an egg shape for the body and a smaller sphere or egg shape for the head. Flexible wires will represent human limbs in the same manner as for the pony.

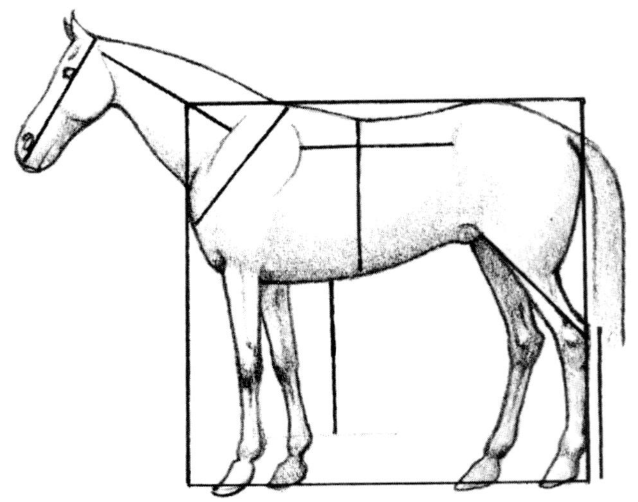

The body of a horse fits roughly into a square. The black lines show how the head length compares with other parts of the body. Some idea of average proportions helps us to make variations of the truth with knowledge of what we are doing.

When drawing figures of any kind, it is important to think about the area of ground on which they stand, otherwise they may look as if they are unstable or falling over. In the case of four-legged animals it is a help at this early stage to join the feet together with light lines to make sure that they appear to be standing solidly on the ground.

There are certain rules about how one should sit on a horse, but these vary in different parts of the world. The cowboy, for example, does not use quite the same seat as a showjumper, and a jockey does not sit like a huntsman. Such details should not be ignored, but you can often get more fun in drawings from riders who have lost contact with the saddle altogether.

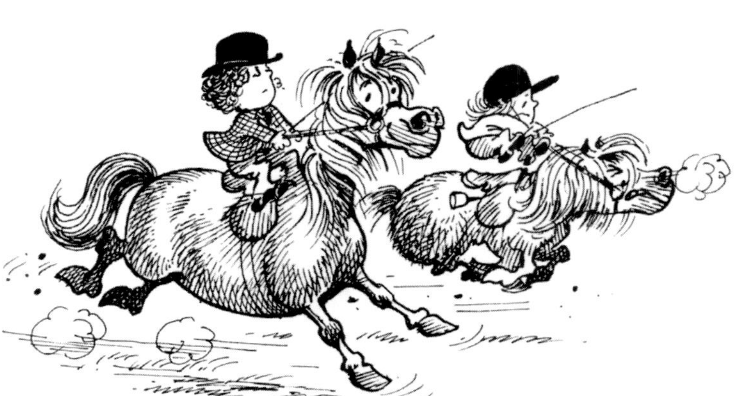

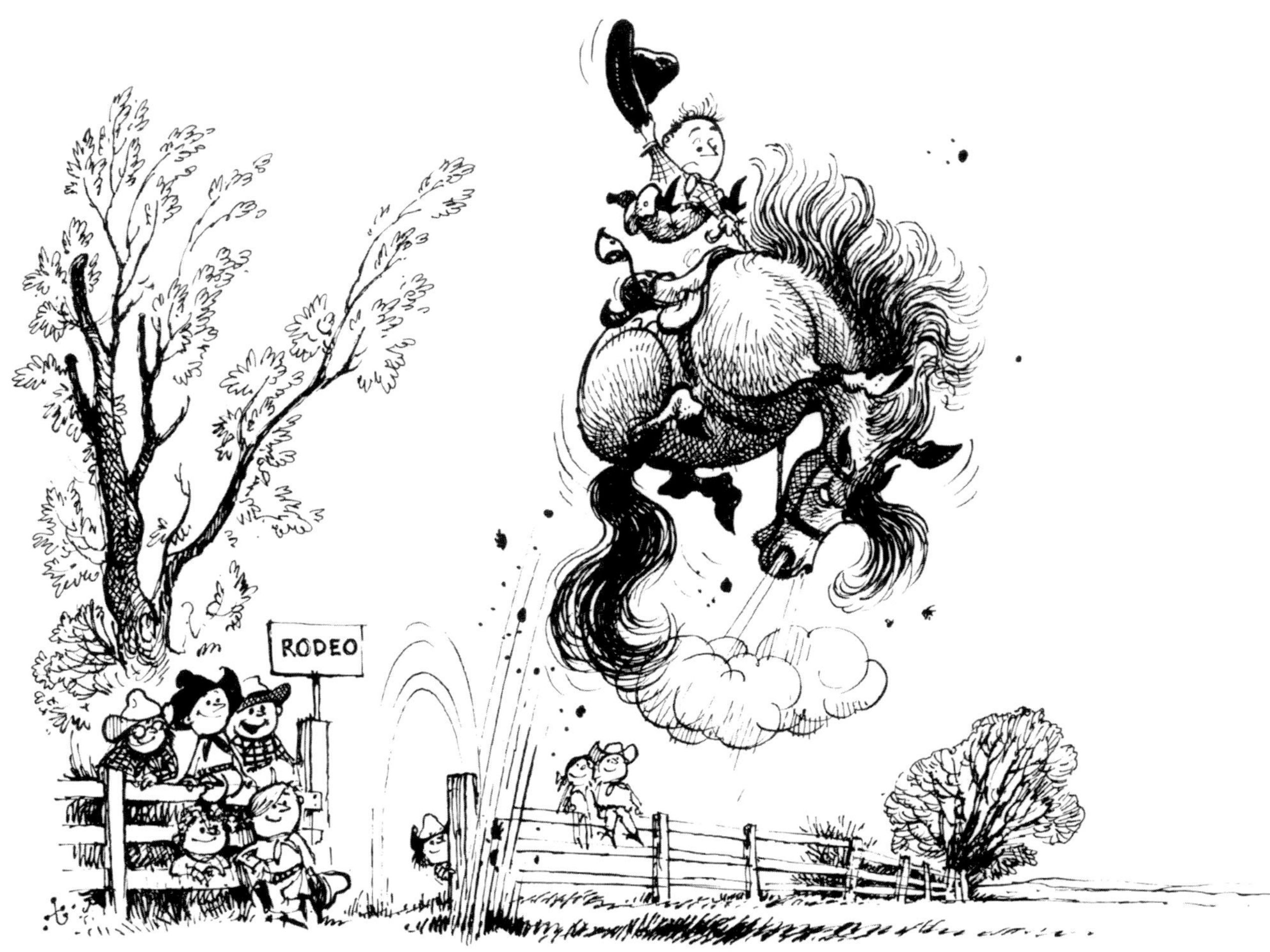
RODEO

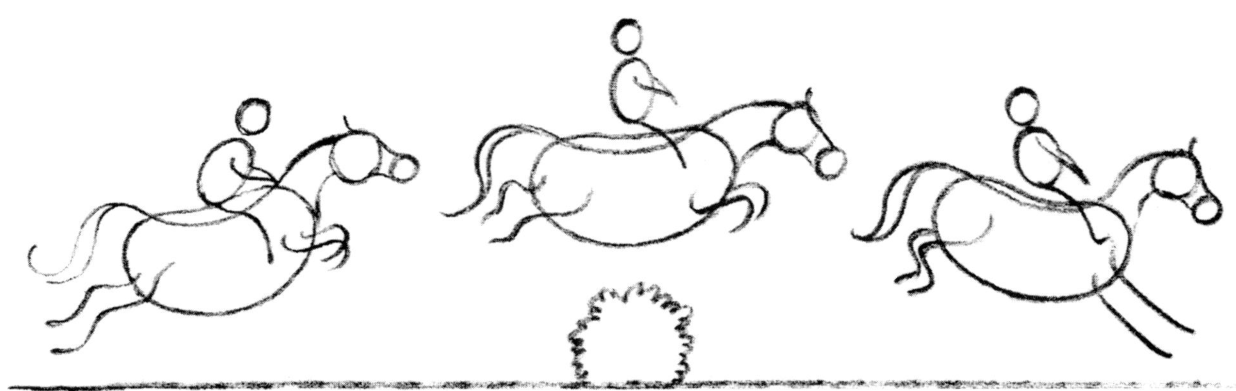

Into action

Movement and action are essential ingredients of a satisfactory drawing. Even if you are drawing a pony which is standing in a more or less static position, there must be a flow of line through the picture to give it life.

You may be creating a fantasy world of your own which does not conform in many ways to real life, but it must nevertheless be a world which is vitally alive in its own way. Indeed you should go further, you should try as an artist to give extra emphasis to the particular kind of movement and action you wish to show.

The feeling of life and speed may be helped at a later stage by the addition of certain details such as flying stones and earth, or a cloud of dust, but by far the most important thing is the arrangement and pattern of your figures on the paper and the first flowing lines on which the picture is built.

Not only is it a mistake to draw detail in the early stages of a composition, but you must not even think in terms of detail. Your whole concentration must be on the movement you wish to express. In the case of animal drawing, the most important single line is often the one which runs from the tip of the nose, over the profile of the head, along the neck and down the back to the end of the tail. Once this line is established, all further lines of action should be in sympathy with it.

The lines of movement do not apply to the pony only, of course. If a rider is present, he is just as important in

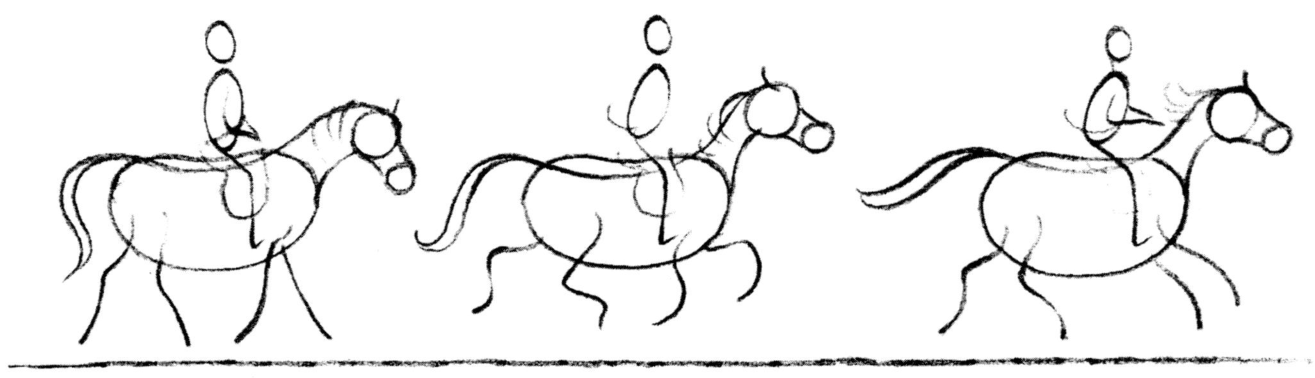

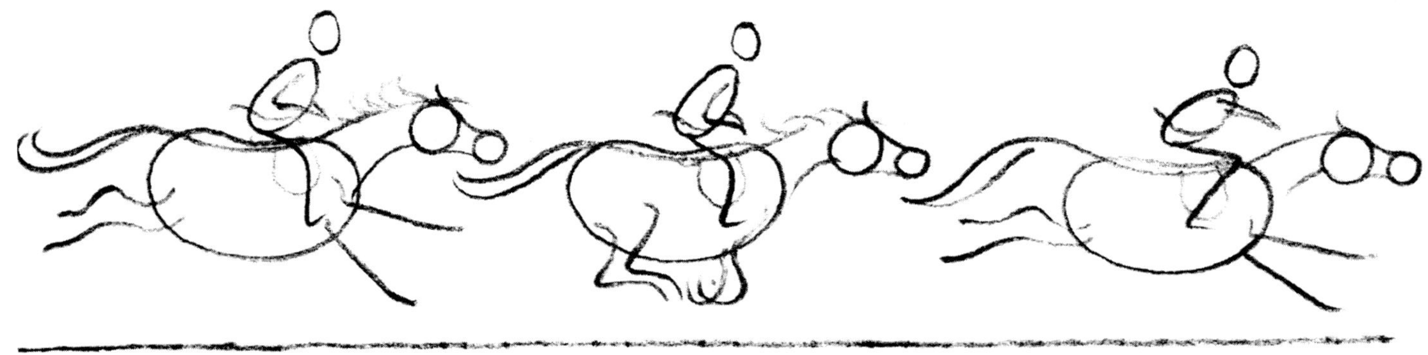

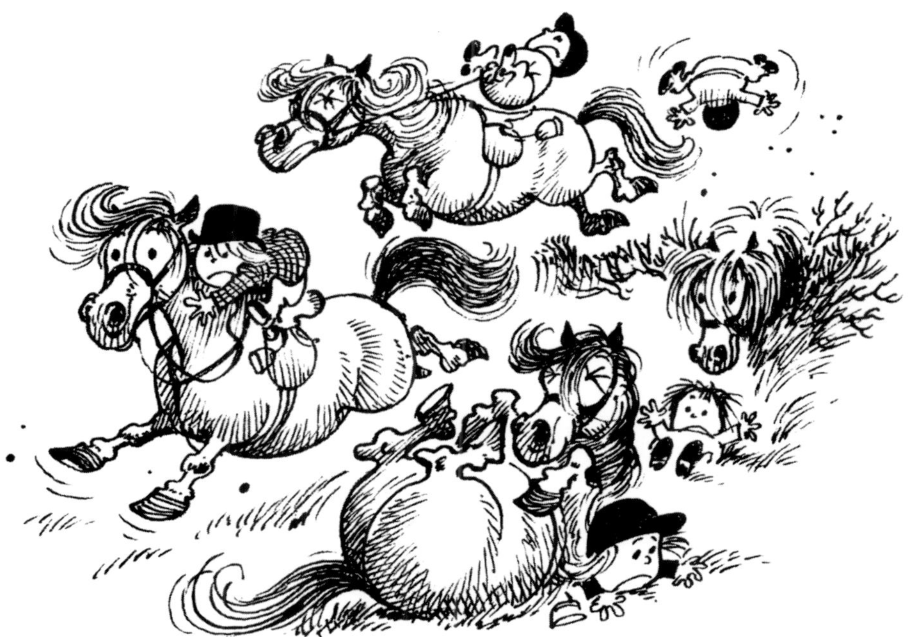

suggesting action and flow. Not only his action but his whole figure must be part of the design of the picture to achieve a satisfactory result.

A first-rate rider in action will of course be nicely balanced on the horse, but when we are making pictures we are concerned not only with the relationship of rider to horse but with the balance of the picture as a whole. We may well be making a drawing where the rider has lost his balance and has achieved anything but a happy relationship with his mount. Nevertheless, both horse and rider must make a happy and balanced shape and pattern on the paper.

With your puppet figures you can work out all these problems long before you get involved in the drawing of any details, and it is less discouraging at this stage if you fail a number of times before you get the effect you are after.

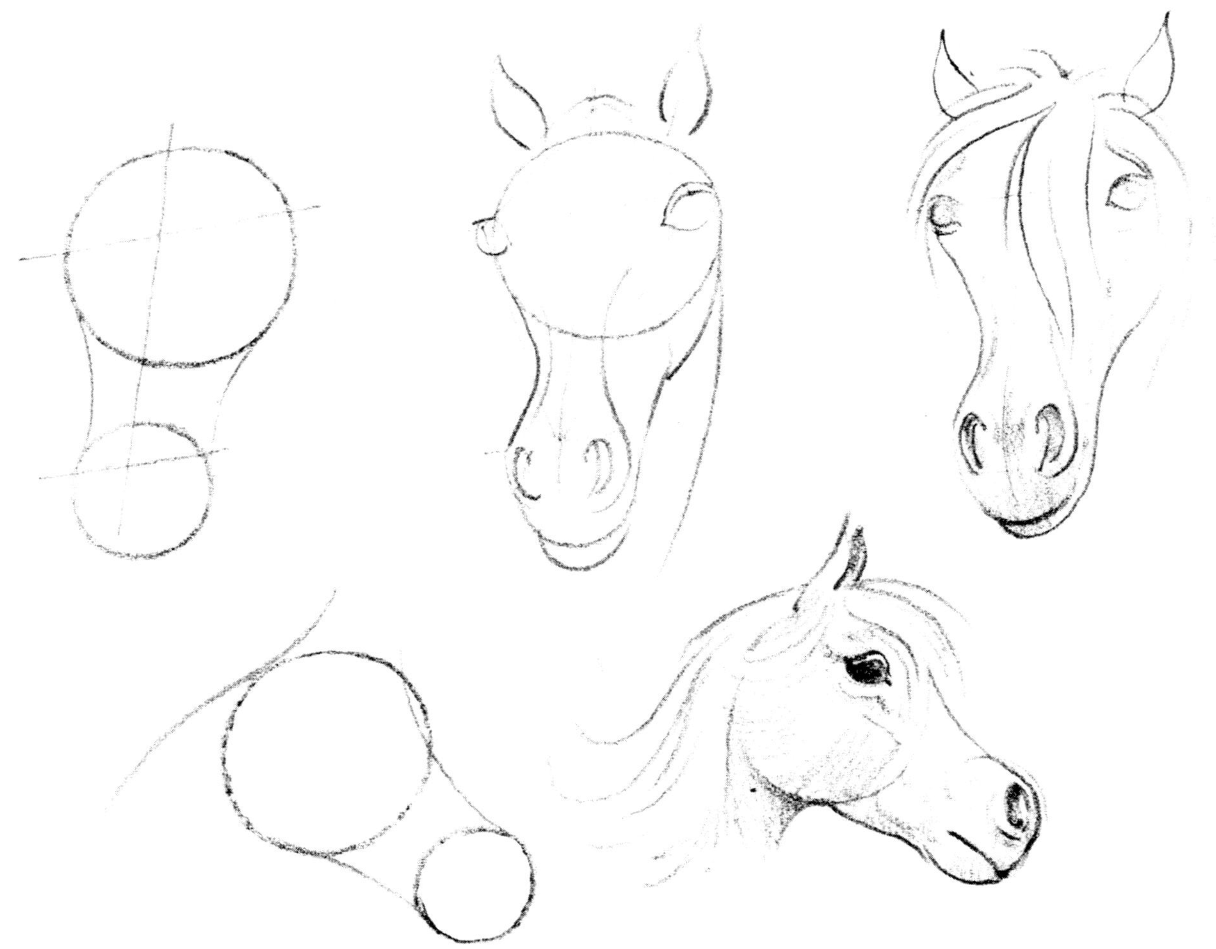

Giving him his head

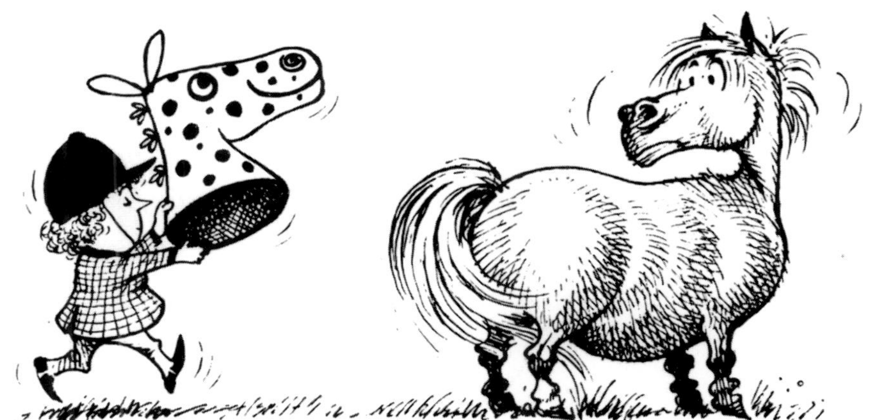

So far we have represented both humans and animals as puppet figures in the simplest form. We have played about with these figures and seen that they are the real bones of our drawings. I hope that you will appreciate what fun may be had with a few bones.

Now we must consider the construction of the pony in more detail. The two spheres which we used to represent the head are a good basis for more careful construction. Draw a line down the centre of the head from the poll between the ears to a point between the nostrils. This will help to get a balanced shape, and a further line crossing it about one-third of the distance from the top will ensure that the eyes are drawn level. Another shorter line can be drawn across in the same way to fix the position of the nostrils.

Try to make drawings from nature of heads and parts of the head as often as possible. This will help you to understand the construction of eyes, nostrils, ears, mouth and so on, but in addition you must practice drawing the head from memory in order thoroughly to assimilate what you have learned. Photographs can also be a great help, because although they may not be so useful in developing drawing techniques, you can at least sit comfortably and study them at times when you may not be able to study the living animal.

Do not draw constantly from photographs, however. Drawing from nature is always better, even if more difficult, both from the point of view of learning to draw well and of learning about horses.

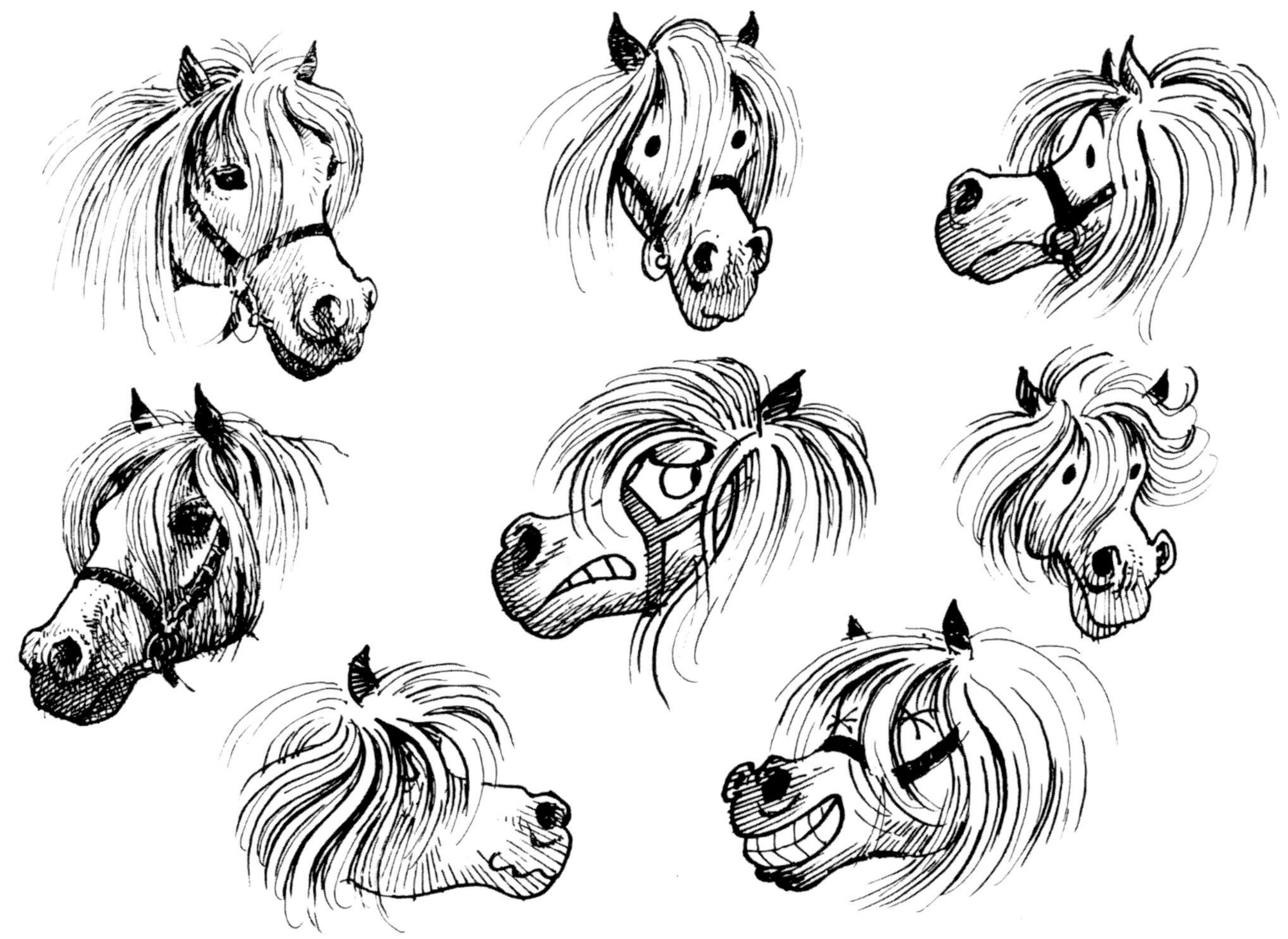

We can create expressions on the face of human beings in a remarkable way by the use of a few very simple tricks. Upturned corners to the mouth will express happiness, pleasure or self-satisfaction, whilst a downward curve will express sadness, annoyance or anger.

The way we represent the eyes as dots, or circles, or slits will also express a great deal, and the position and form of the eyebrows can have quite surprising effects. When we combine all these in their various forms, we have an endless variety of facial expressions which are the stock-in-trade of the cartoonist.

In showing the feelings and emotions of ponies, and indeed of any animal, the same method can be used. Remember, however, that animals are not human, even if humans are animals, and they cannot laugh or cry in real life. Although in the world of our imagination we can make our animals behave exactly as we choose, yet we must beware of taking things to the point where we destroy their essential animal characteristics.

Compared to the human version, the nostrils of horses are large, mobile and very expressive. The value of nostrils in human expression is to some extent limited by their relatively small size and lack of mobility, but in the case of the pony they are one of the most valuable points to seize upon because they are so characteristic.

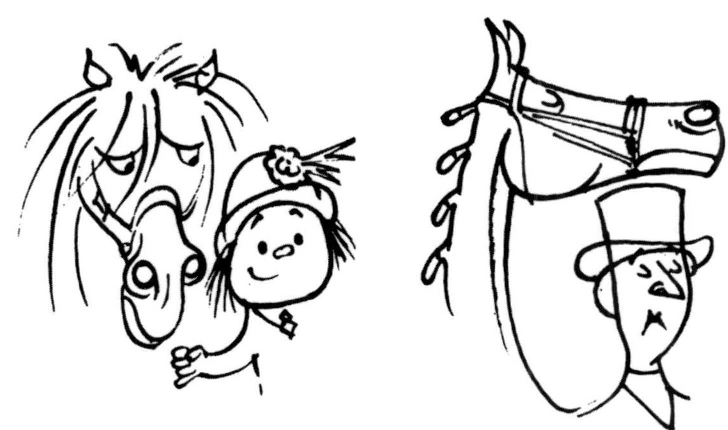

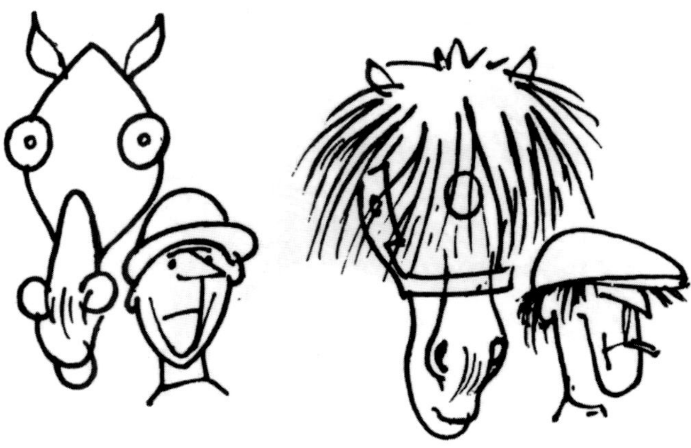

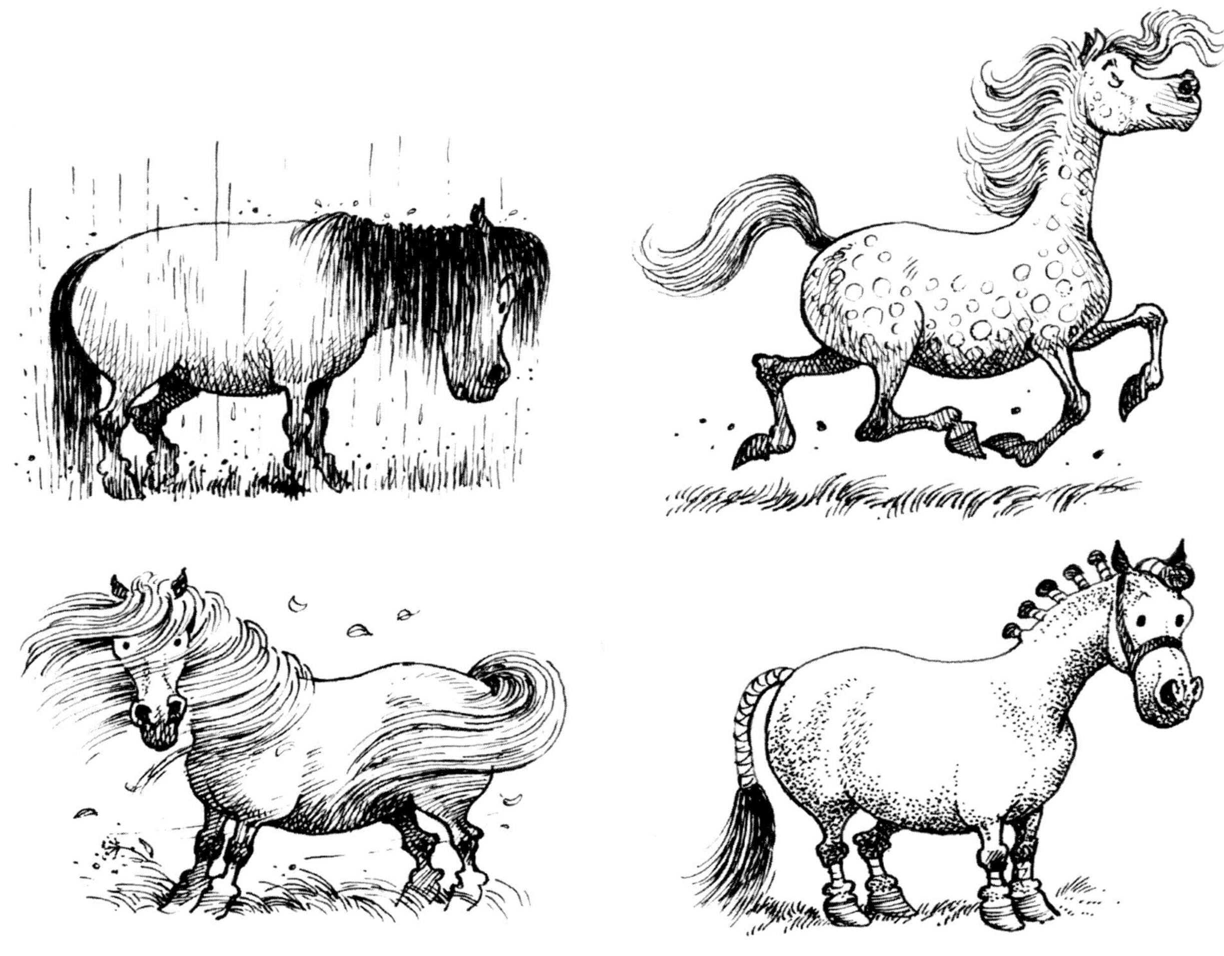

Pony tail

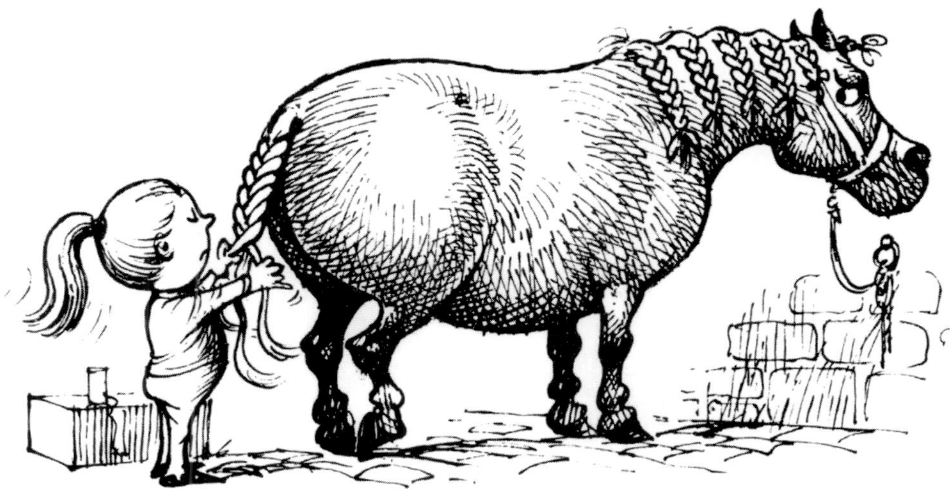

The tail and mane of a pony are very important indeed, not only to him for flicking off flies and keeping them out of his eyes, but also to us when we come to draw him.

The way the hair flows or hangs can suggest a great deal about the creature. It can be a valuable indication of his emotional state or medical condition, or just of his mood of the moment. Its texture and position can also help greatly in suggesting external conditions such as wind or rain or the irritation of insects on a hot afternoon.

They can also help very much in suggesting speed, movement and actions of all kinds, because the loose hair is so mobile by comparison with the more solid parts of the body. This contrast between the hair and the rounded, solid form of the body and legs is also very important in that it gives us most useful textures and patterns to play with in our drawings, and makes our pictures more interesting, varied and pleasing.

A dark tail and mane on a lighter pony or lighter hair against a darker body can produce the most pleasing pictorial possibilities, whilst the hair texture itself can produce the most interesting contrast with the glossy surface of a well-groomed animal or the varied materials of riding clothes and tack.

Bandaged tails and plaited manes are also interesting in shape and pattern and add to the endless possibilities of picture making.

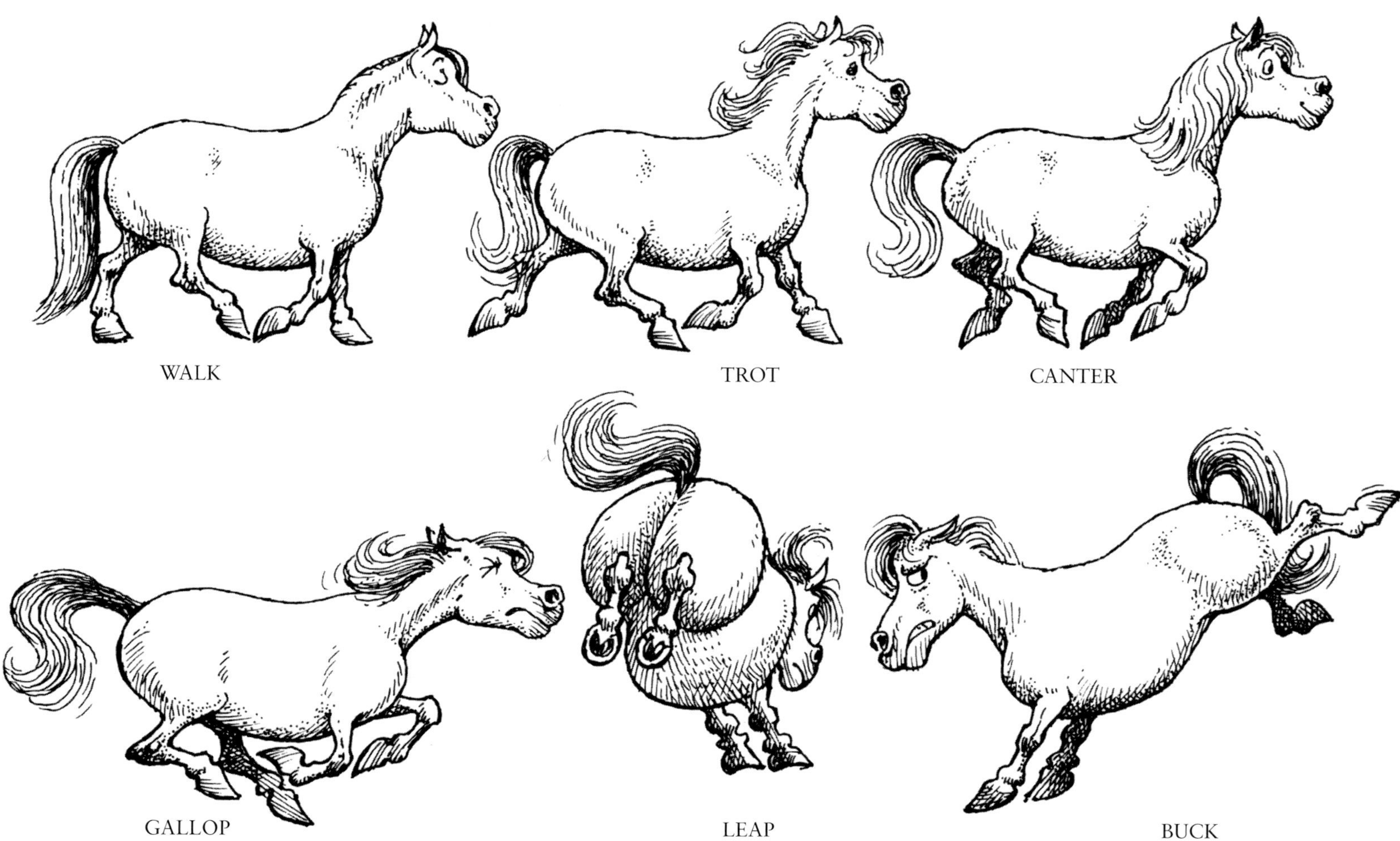

WALK
TROT
CANTER
GALLOP
LEAP
BUCK

Legs to stand on

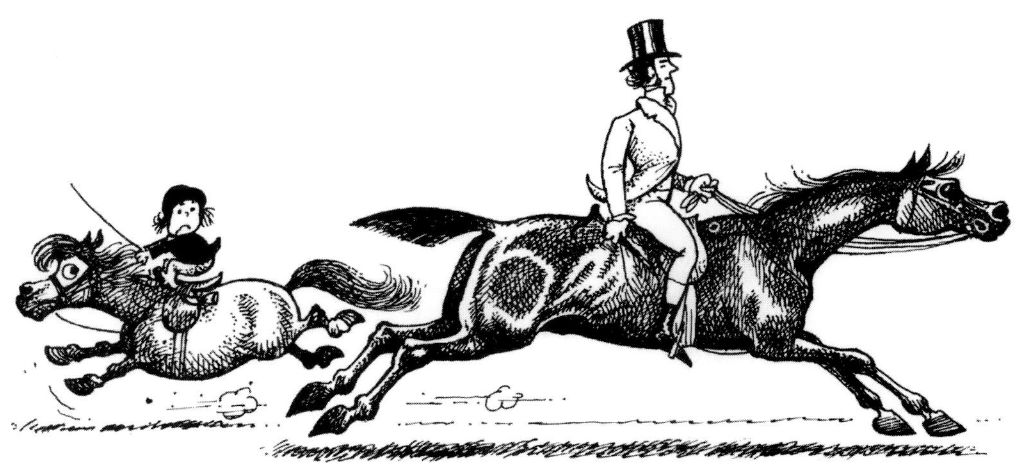

The sequence in which a horse moves its legs when in motion is very difficult to follow and to understand by simply watching horses in action, particularly when they are moving quickly.

If you look at old sporting prints, which are drawings made before the invention of photography, you will see that although man had been closely associated with horses for hundreds of years, he did not fully understand their action, particularly at the gallop.

The result was that galloping horses were represented as having their legs stretched out in front and behind in the stiff unnatural manner of a rocking horse. The invention of photography changed all this. By taking many individual pictures of a horse in action, from the walk through the trot and canter to the gallop, it was soon possible to study the natural sequence of leg movements and to understand them exactly.

The slow-motion camera has made this even easier to follow and to understand, and you should take every opportunity of studying the movements of horses from photographs. However, although photographs show the correct movements, they do not always appear to do so, and certain individual photographs may not suggest smooth movement and action at all. It is up to you to learn and then select from the knowledge acquired. It is more important to give an impression of rhythmic natural action than to worry too much about reality.

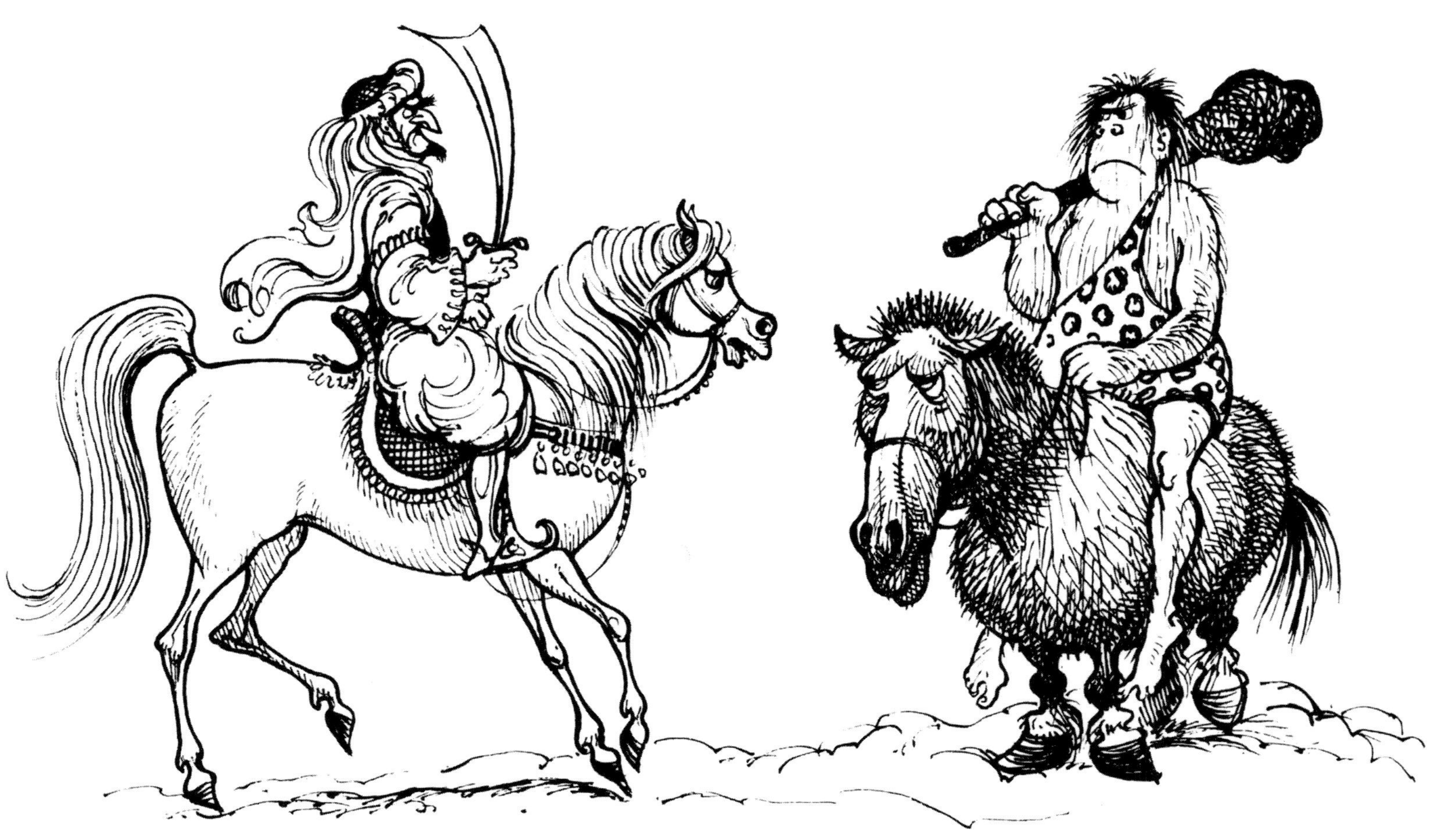

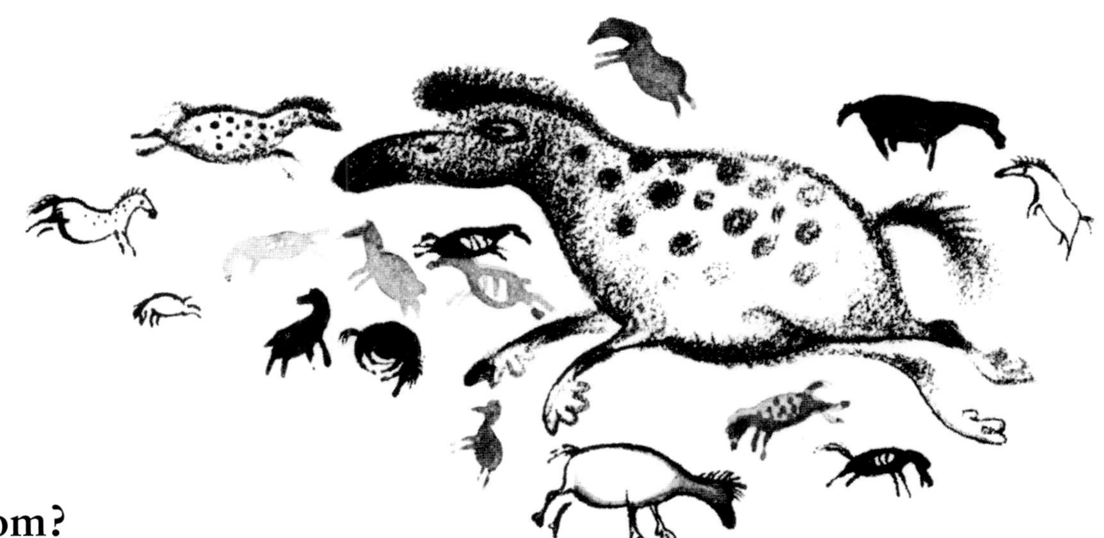

Where did he come from?

The earliest ancestor of the horse is now generally accepted as being a creature called *Eohippus* or the Dawn Horse. He is known also as *Hyracotherium*, but I'm not sure that it matters to us very much.

The important thing is that he was a small mammal about the size of a dog, and he had three toes on his hind feet and four on his front. He was succeeded in the course of time by a rather larger animal with three toes on each foot, and later still by an even larger creature who had the same number of toes but insisted on running on the centre ones only. At some later date an animal developed whose toes, all except the centre ones, were hidden under the skin, and he was succeeded in his turn by the modern type of horse with its characteristic hoof.

These facts, whether strictly true or not, are enough to illustrate how the horse came to have only one toe. Zebras and asses are also members of the horse family, but there are not many truly wild horses in existence today.

We are concerned mainly with the domesticated horse as we know him today. Broadly speaking, the horses we know can be divided up into two main sections, the Northern or cold-blooded group and the Southern or hot-blooded group.

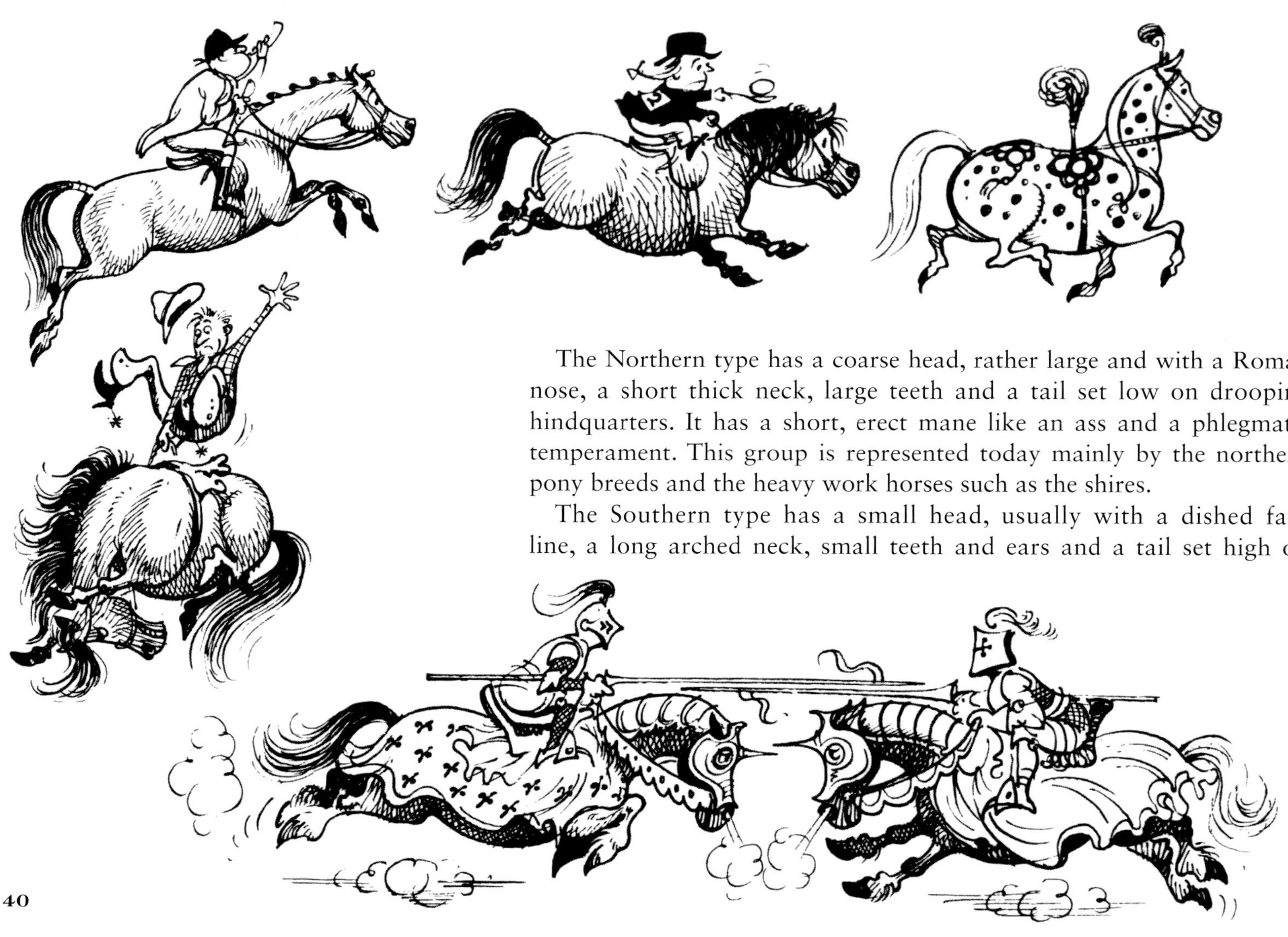

The Northern type has a coarse head, rather large and with a Roman nose, a short thick neck, large teeth and a tail set low on drooping hindquarters. It has a short, erect mane like an ass and a phlegmatic temperament. This group is represented today mainly by the northern pony breeds and the heavy work horses such as the shires.

The Southern type has a small head, usually with a dished face line, a long arched neck, small teeth and ears and a tail set high on

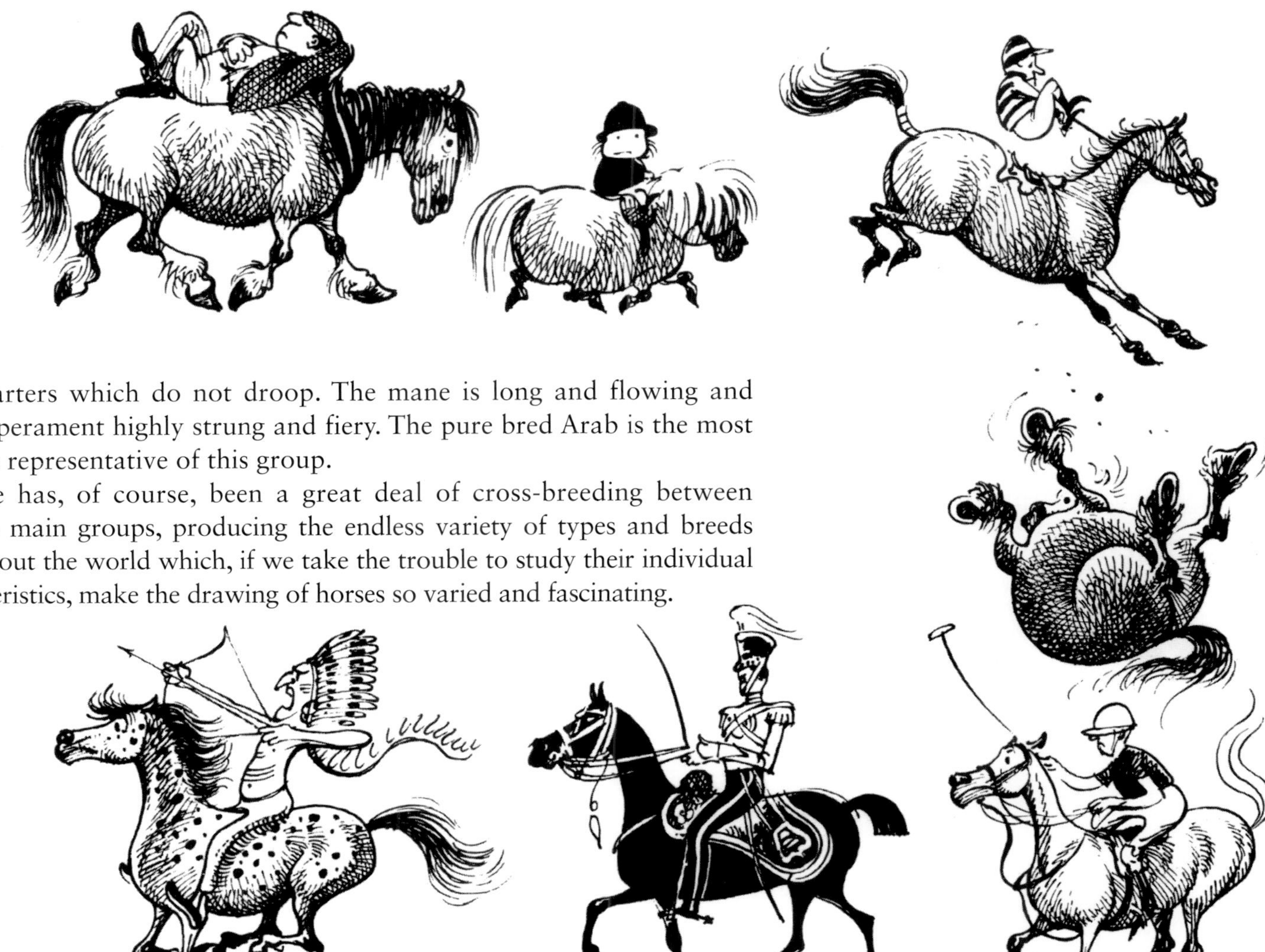

hindquarters which do not droop. The mane is long and flowing and the temperament highly strung and fiery. The pure bred Arab is the most obvious representative of this group.

There has, of course, been a great deal of cross-breeding between the two main groups, producing the endless variety of types and breeds throughout the world which, if we take the trouble to study their individual characteristics, make the drawing of horses so varied and fascinating.

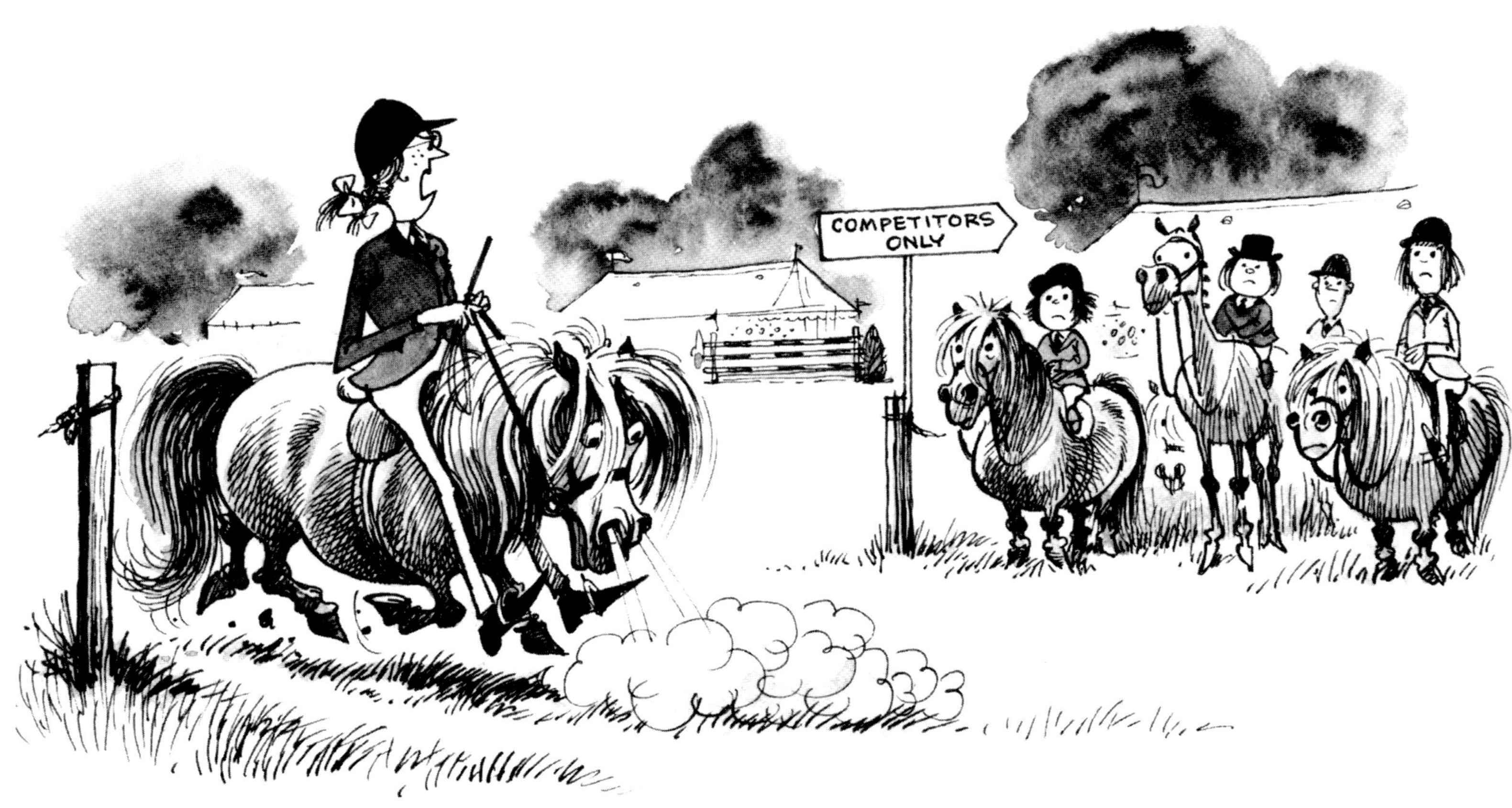

'He knocked down the last fence – with my foot.'

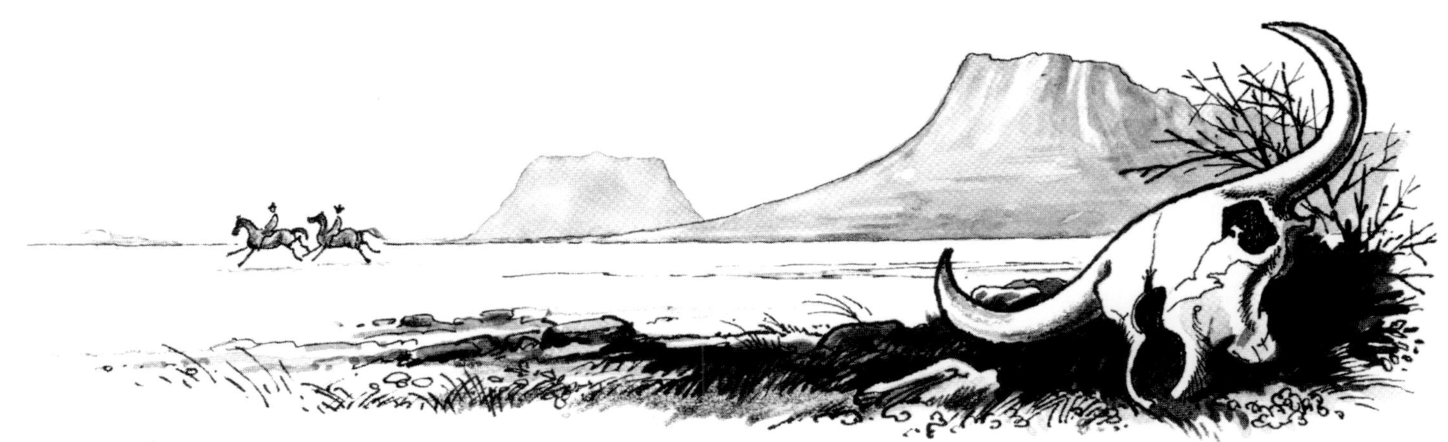

Riding country

However well you may draw animals, if they are set in an unconvincing background the results will be disastrous. Whether the surroundings be detailed and full of interest, or the briefest suggestion of space, the drawing must never be skimped.

We have already seen that the sketchbook is our most valuable asset in acquiring knowledge of ponies and of improving our drawing skill. It is just as invaluable when it comes to the drawing of landscape and settings of all kinds.

You may wish to take all kinds of liberties in the creation of your pictures, and there is no rule which says that your backgrounds must be realistic in treatment. This is a matter for each individual to work out for himself and to interpret through his imagination and invention.

Your imaginative efforts are, however, unlikely to be convincing unless they are based on sound knowledge and careful drawing.

Notes should be made at every opportunity of anything and everything which may be useful to you, from mountains to molehills and from trees to grasses. Your sketchbook will become an endless supply of patterns, shapes and textures which will be most useful when making pictures.

Unless you are lucky enough to have a natural feeling for perspective, it can be a complicated subject of study and we do not have the space to go deeply into it here.

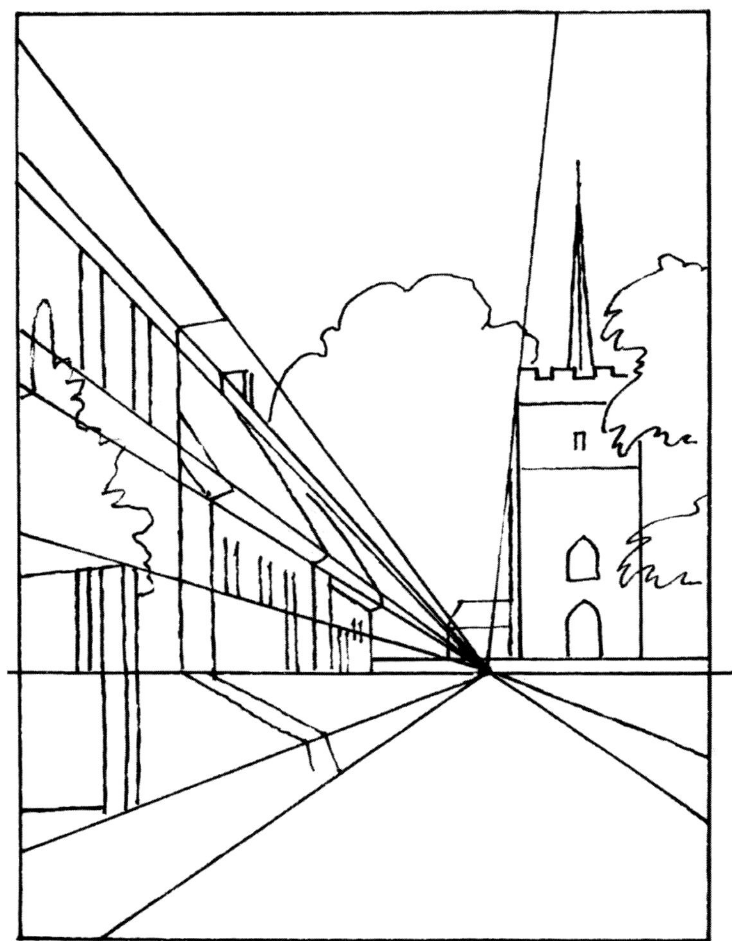 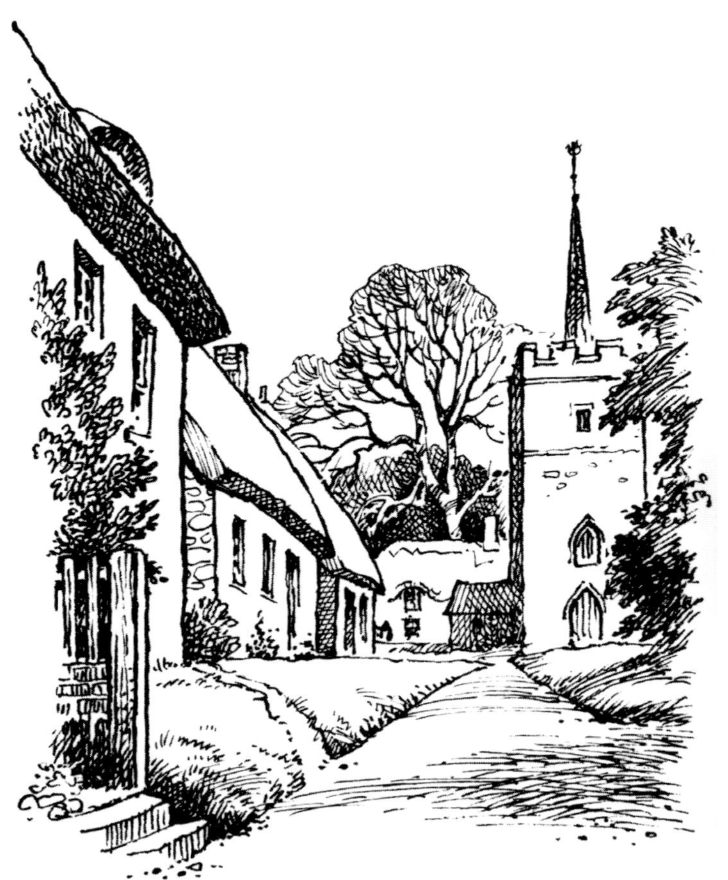

Briefly, however, when starting a drawing, you should decide upon your eye level first and a faint pencil line drawn across the paper will fix this vital level. Everything above this line will slope down towards it, and everything below it will slope upwards towards it. The point on the eye level where the lines meet is called the vanishing point. We may have one or more vanishing points on the eye level line. Dramatic effects can often be achieved by making the eye level unusually low or high on the paper, as this gives the effect of looking up at or down on our subject.

For general purposes, however, the eye level in a picture will pass through the heads of human figures when standing up, because of course this is roughly the level of the eyes of the artist.

Before we leave the subject of background, it should be said that photography can help us just as much here as in learning about horses themselves. We may not wish to confine ourselves to drawing horses in the limited localities in which we live or travel. The world is a big and varied place, and even in this modern world it is not easy to journey to the prairies of America to draw cowboys or to the steppes of Russia to get backgrounds for Cossacks. Even if you are lucky enough to travel widely, it is unlikely that you can go everywhere where there are horses. It is very useful, therefore, to make a collection of photographs and clippings from magazines and newspapers of interesting backgrounds and settings.

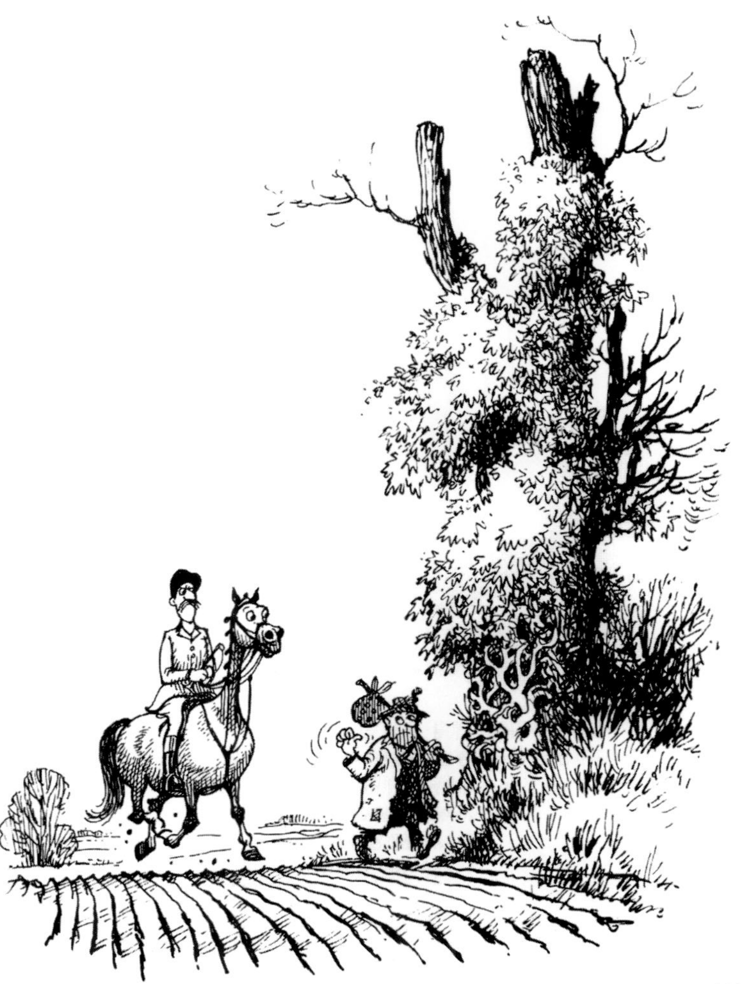

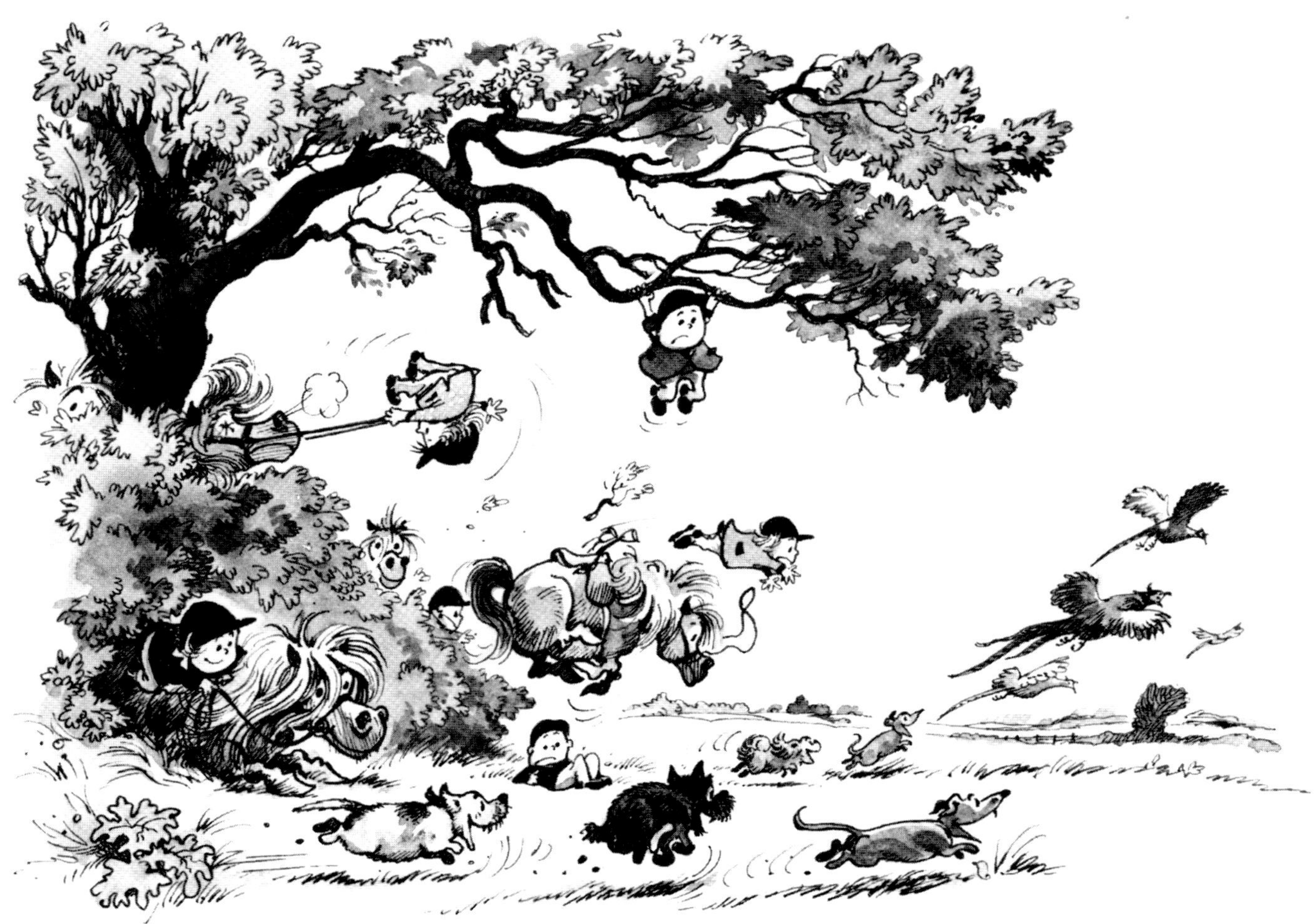

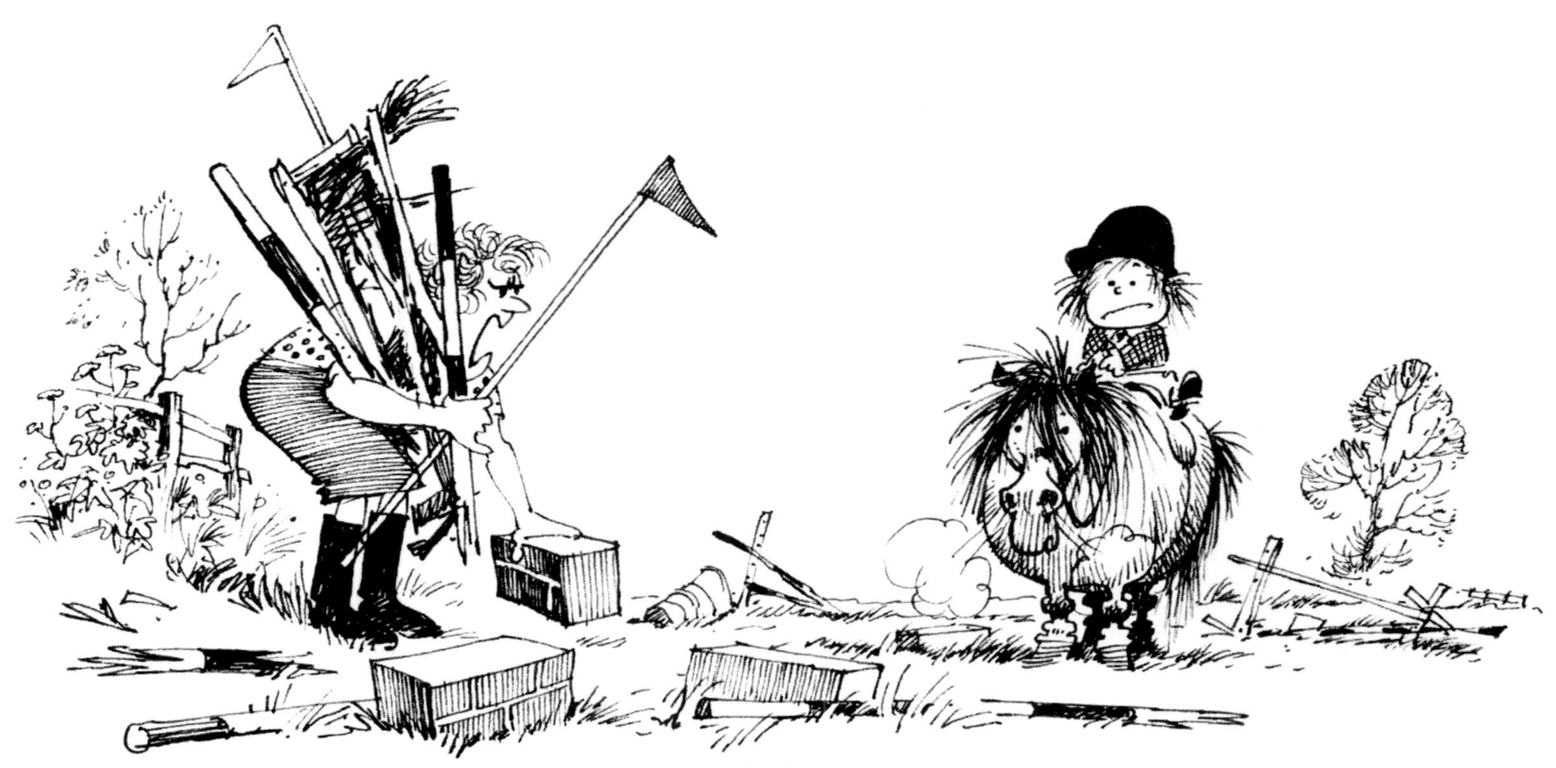

'I don't suppose Princess Anne expects *her* mother to keep tidying up after her.'

The Australian outback, the inside of the big top at the circus, the hunting country of Europe or the pampas of South America – any of these settings and a million more may be the backgrounds you require. Use photographs for reference, but *never* neglect drawing from life in your sketchbook.

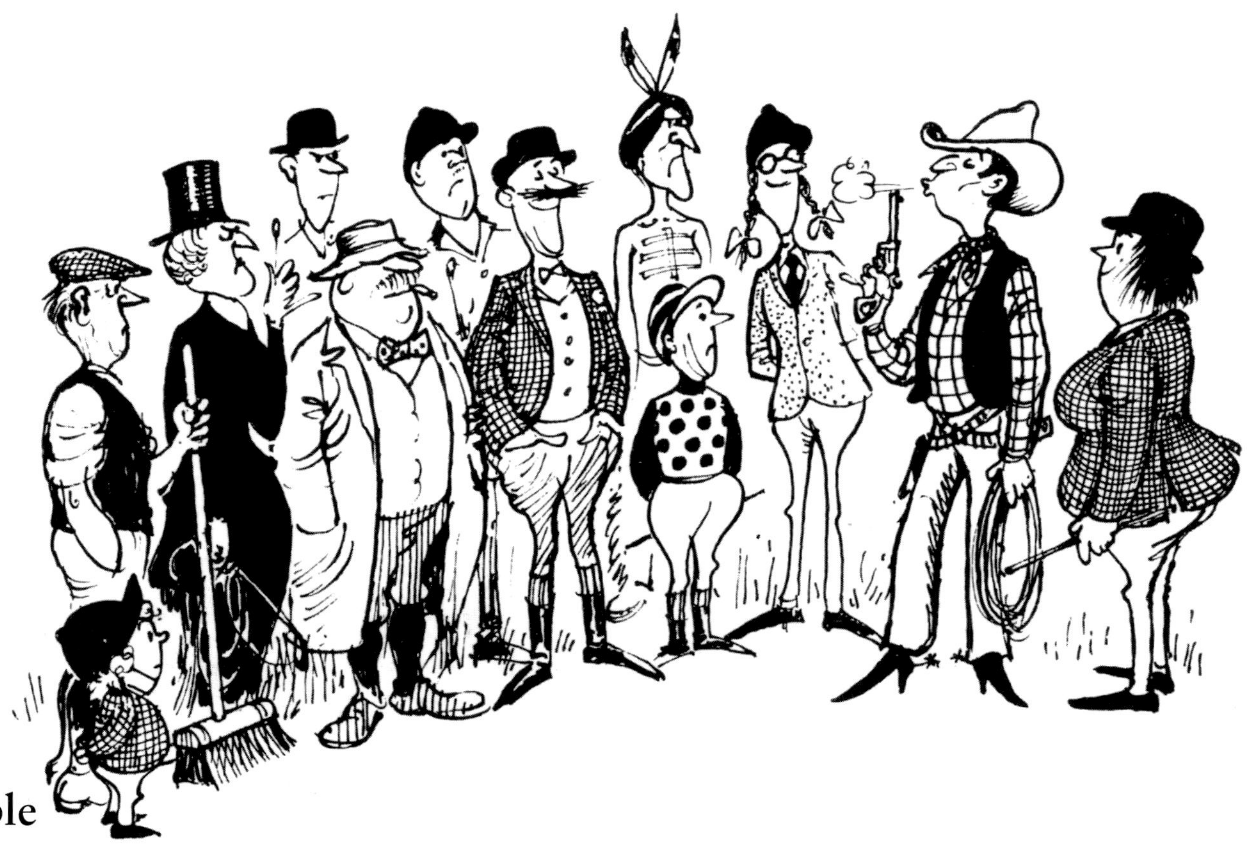

Horsey people

In spite of the fact that men have been falling off horses and being bitten by them for countless ages, a bond of friendship exists between them which is astonishing to say the least. So complete is this link, that it is difficult to think about horses without also thinking about horsey people. These types are even more numerous, if anything, than the types of horses, and they are rich material indeed for our purpose.

Showjumping arenas are not only full of them but are also surrounded by them. There are the competitors themselves, from the red-faced sporting colonels to the tiny enthusiasts who must be lifted into the saddle. There are the spectators who watch them, from the doting mothers to the critical connoisseurs, and all are fascinated by everything from the winning of a rosette to the breaking of a collar bone.

The hunting field provides a rich vein of characters to explore and use, and so do the dealers, horse doctors, blacksmiths, riding mistresses and equitation experts of all kinds.

The racecourses are crammed with horsey people, from the jockeys and stable lads to the elegantly dressed racegoers and down-at-heel tipsters.

There are cowboys and gauchos, cavalry soldiers in richly elaborate uniform and circus performers in spangled tights. And of course many others.

Many of these people we can meet and get down in our sketchbooks, but others we cannot, so again we must make use of photographs and pictures of all kinds.

Even photographs cannot tell us much about the horsemen of early days, the knights in armour, the mounted hordes of Genghis Khan, the Crusaders and coachmen, but other artists have gathered the information and reconstructed the clothing and trappings, and this is one way at least in which history books can be fascinating.

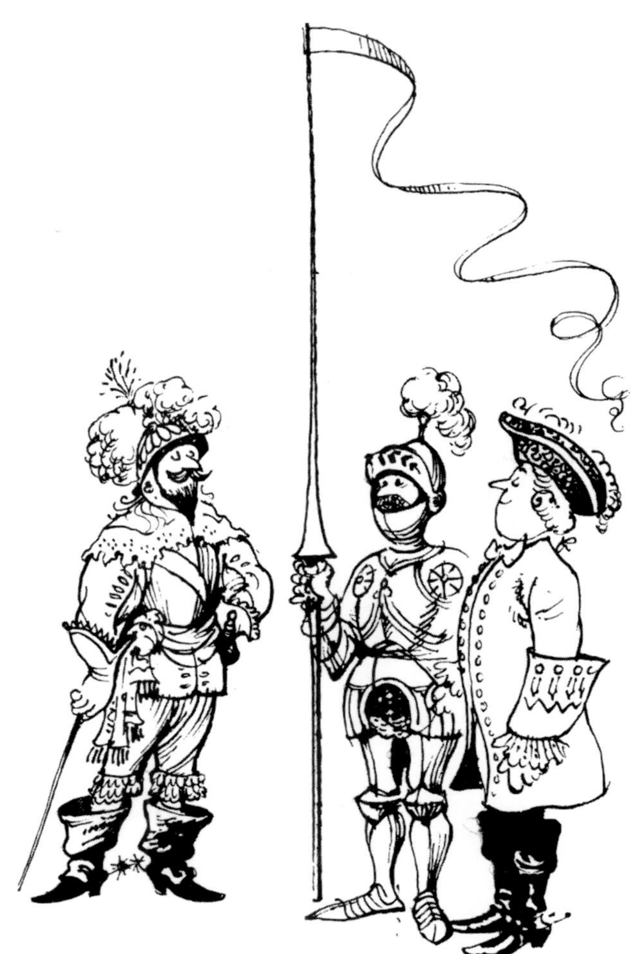

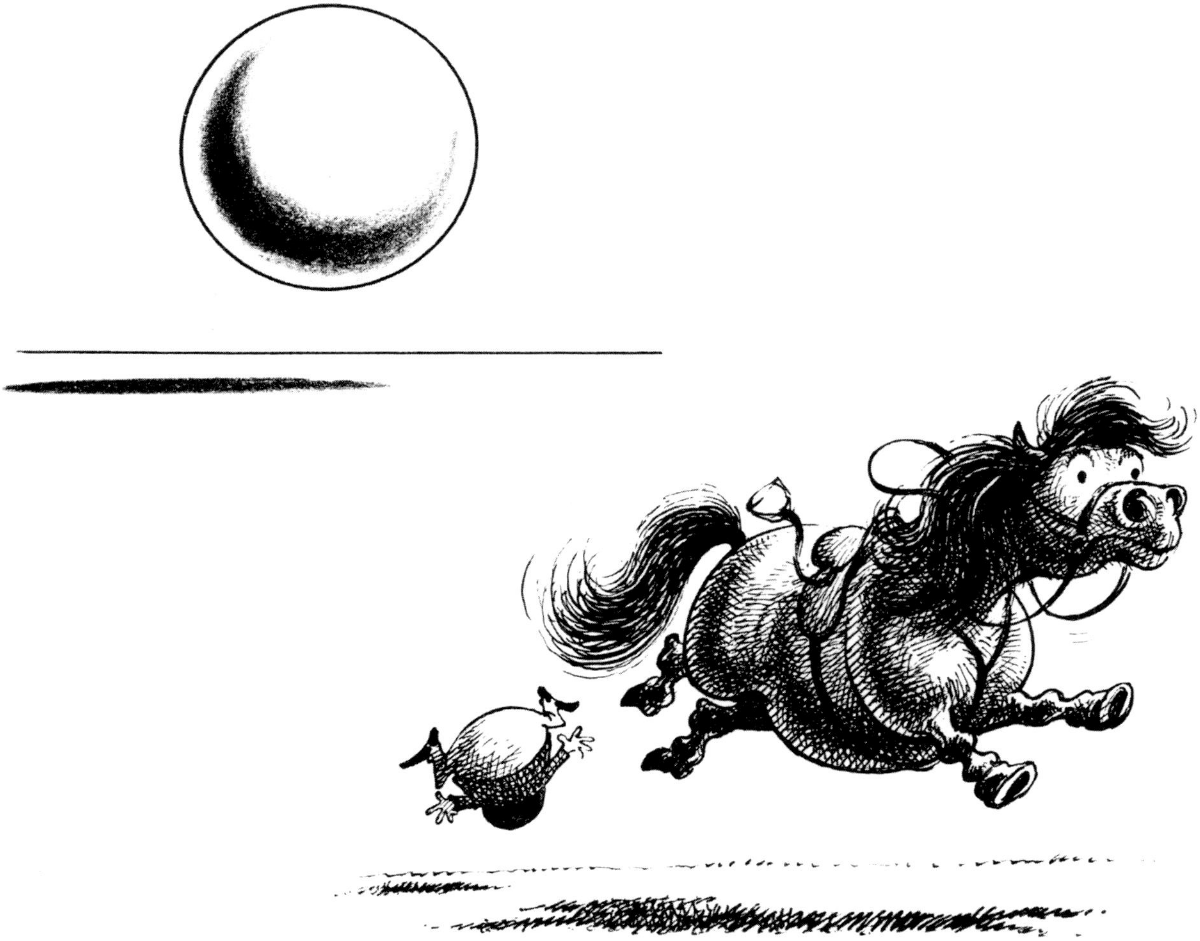

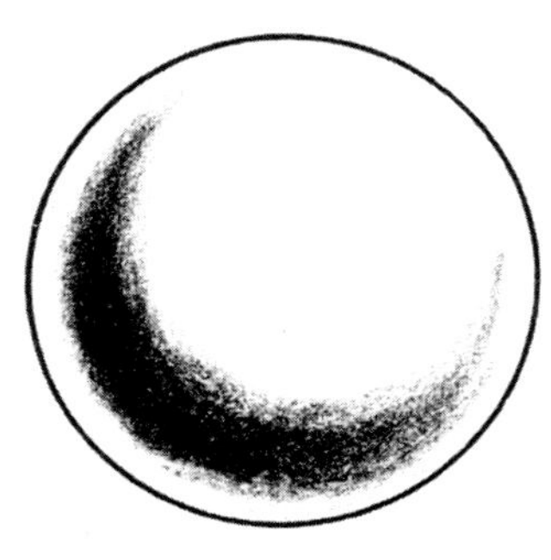

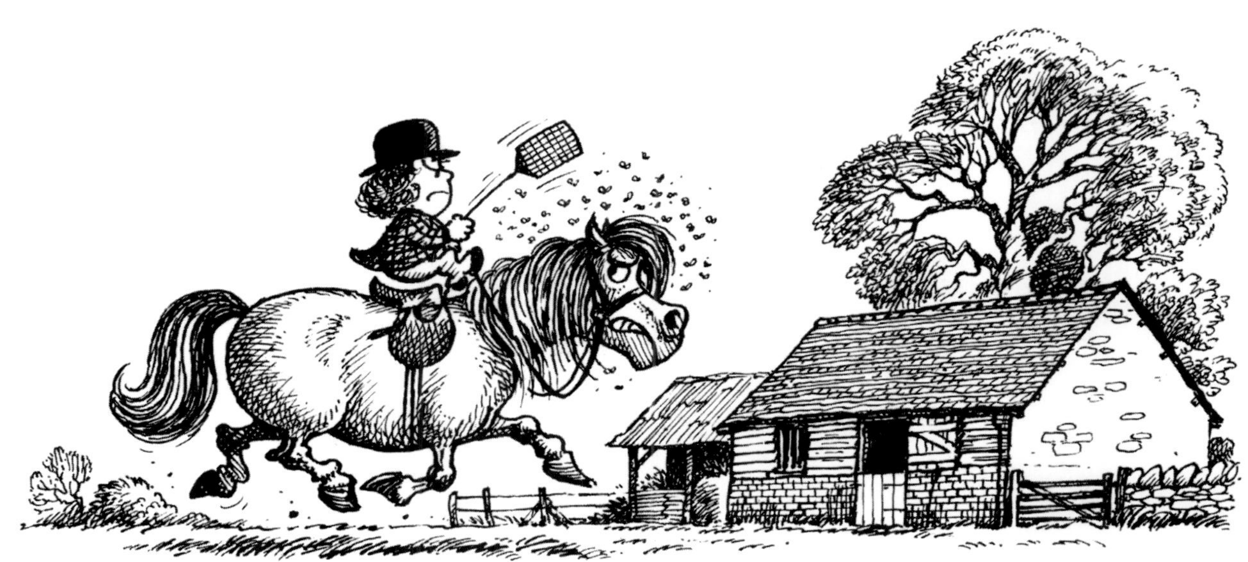

On form

It is the effect of light falling on to objects and being reflected off them again that makes them appear solid. To achieve an effect of solidity and mass in your drawings, therefore, you must first decide from which direction the main source of light is coming. Surfaces facing in this direction will obviously be light, and those facing away from it will be relatively darker.

In most cases light will be reflected back again from the ground surface and other objects on to the darker surfaces of the object you are dealing with, and this helps enormously to show the three-dimensional form. By fixing the main direction of light, you can also work out the size and shape of the shadows which will be cast by an object on to the ground and on to other objects nearby.

Most objects in your drawings will have surface texture of one kind or another; hair, cloth, stone, brick, leaves, grass and so on. Use these surface textures not only to record facts but also to give variety and interest

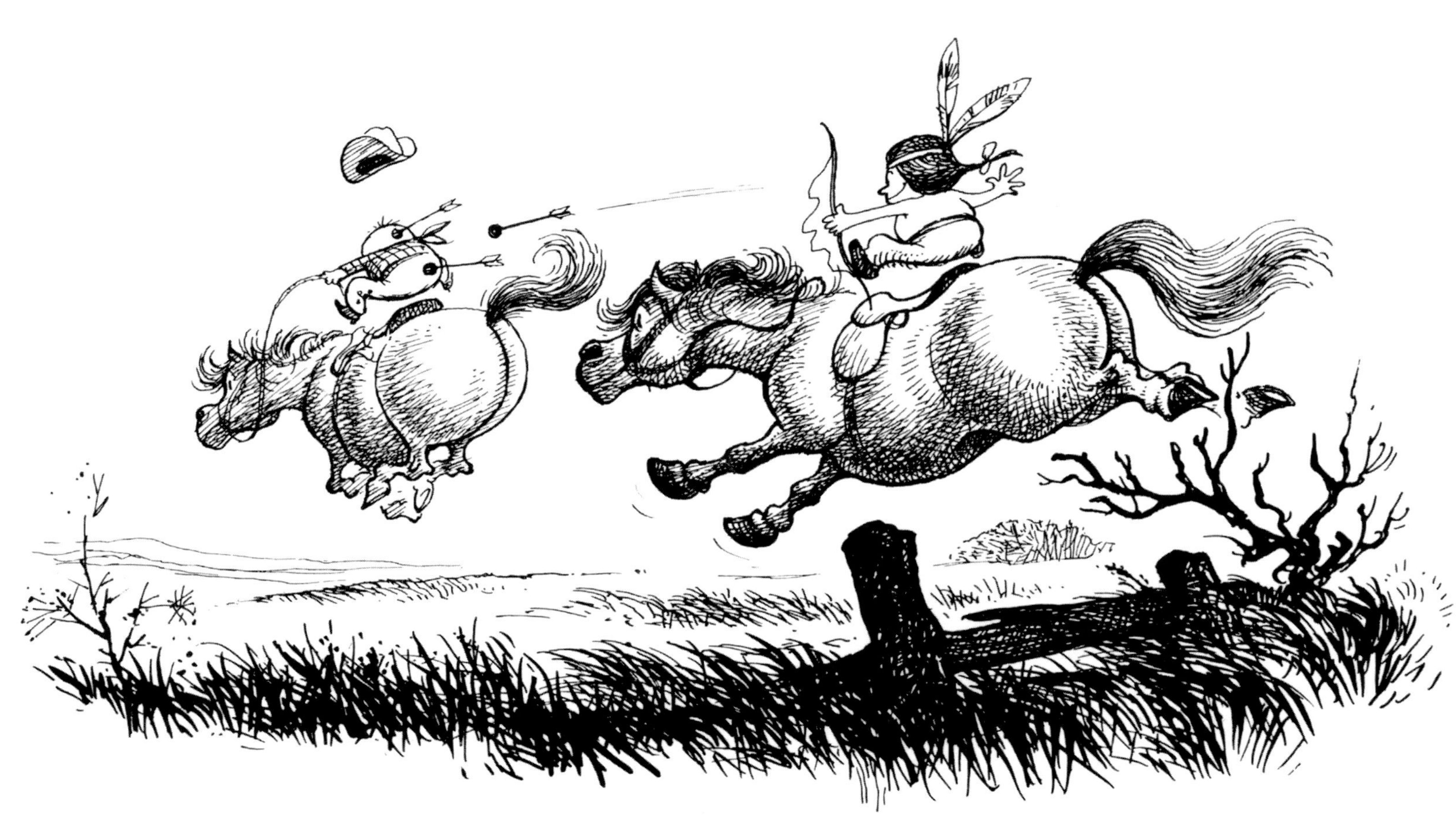

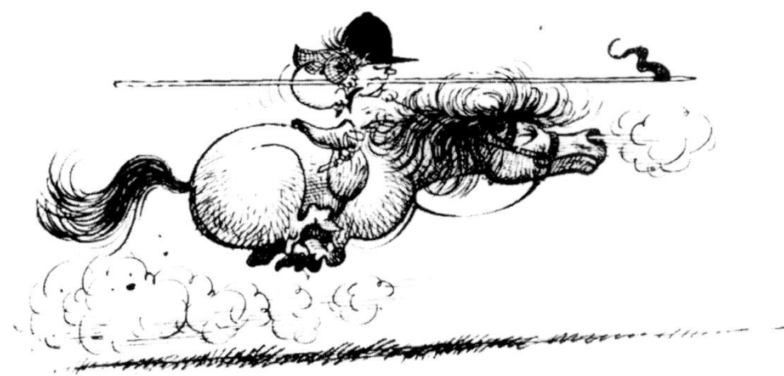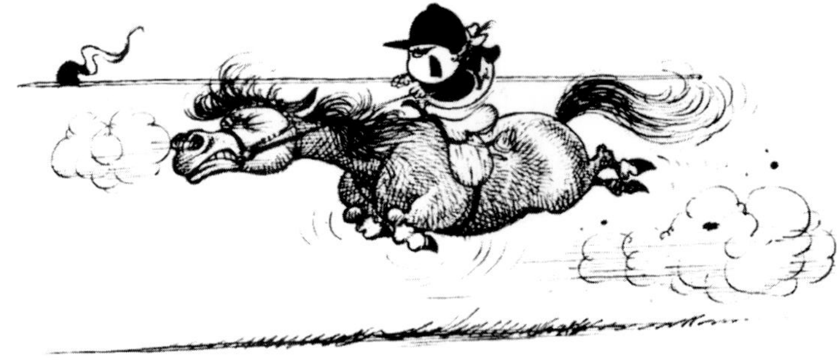

Fountain pen drawing from *Thelwell's Riding Academy*.

to your picture. When suggesting these materials in a drawing, do so carefully and in the right places and the textures themselves will produce tones and shadows which will make the drawing look solid and three-dimensional.

We have touched briefly on perspective in the geometrical sense earlier, but there is another aspect of perspective which must be dealt with. This is sometimes referred to as 'aerial perspective' because it is concerned with creating a sense of space and distance between objects in a drawing or painting.

We have all noticed at one time or another (particularly when looking across open landscape) how objects far away from our eyes appear not only smaller but paler in tone than objects in the foreground. Strong lights and darks and colours merge gradually towards grey as they get further away. This is due to the increasing amount of air between the objects and our eye.

It is relatively easy when using colour or washes of tone in a picture to suggest this illusion of space, but when only black line is being used it is harder to deal with.

The effect can, however, be created by the relative weight of line used for objects in a picture. Foreground objects should be drawn with a relatively strong, bold treatment. Objects in the middle distance should have a lighter touch and thinner line, and if any solid blacks are used at this distance they should be kept to a minimum. The far distance will be suggested with a finer line still, and no solid blacks used at all.

It also helps if some white paper shows between the linework of the objects in the foreground and the finer lines of distant objects, so that they do not quite touch each other.

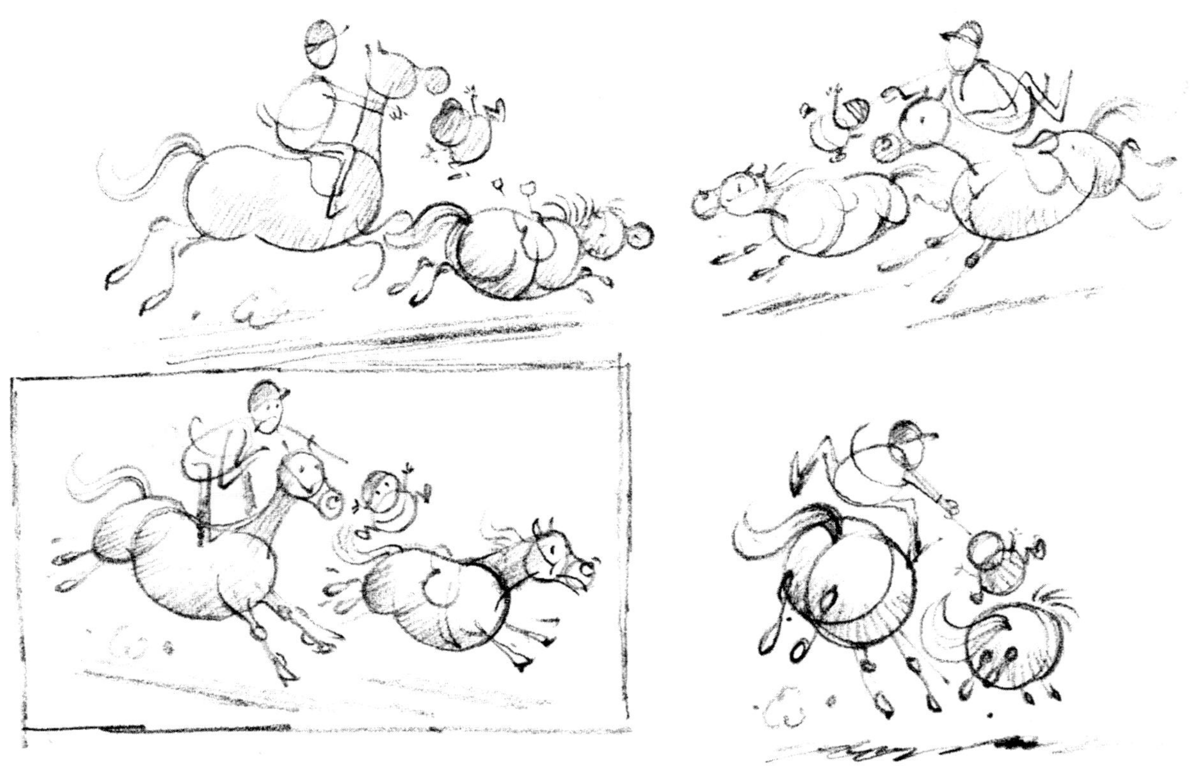

Stage I

On the opposite page we have set ourselves a problem and have decided what we are going to draw. Now we must work out our composition. At this stage we are not concerned with detail remember, but with finding a design which will put over the facts clearly and in as interesting a way as possible.

First, make a number of little drawings of the situation on rough paper. Try different angles and points of view but keep your sketches small, bold and simple. Work on them until you feel you have tried all the approaches to the subject. Then choose the one you like best and think about it very carefully.

54

The finishing line

It may be of interest to take a problem of illustration and work out the stages necessary to arrive at a finished drawing.

In this case we wish to illustrate a situation where a child has neglected to pay her fee or 'cap' for a day's hunting, and the hunt secretary is keen to collect his dues.

We are creating the characters, so it is up to us to decide how they will behave. Before we can think about composition, we must decide how the secretary will get to grips with Sandra and her money.

He could perhaps put the hounds on to her. That's an idea! But in order to get a pack of hounds into the size of page we are allowed, we would have to make our main characters rather small. He must obviously run her to earth because we know her – and so does he – and she will be deaf to any sounds she doesn't want to hear. When he catches up with her, how will he stop her? No lasso in the hunting field. But wait! That handle on his hunting crop will hook nicely round a field gate, or most other objects when necessary. His problem is solved – now for ours.

We want to tell the whole story in one picture. The chase, the closing in, the moment of truth. We have made a start on the previous page. Let us continue overleaf.

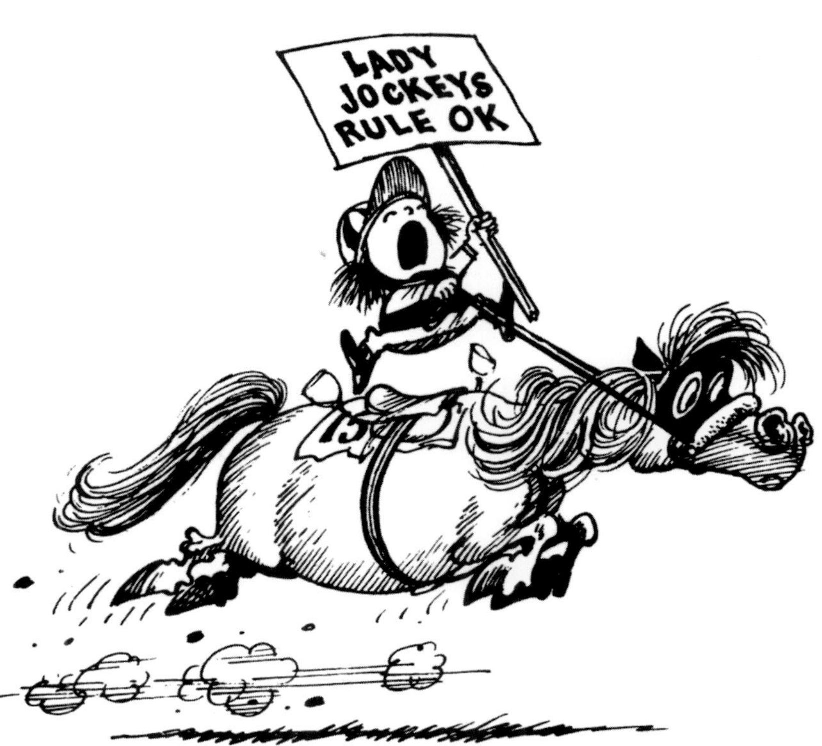

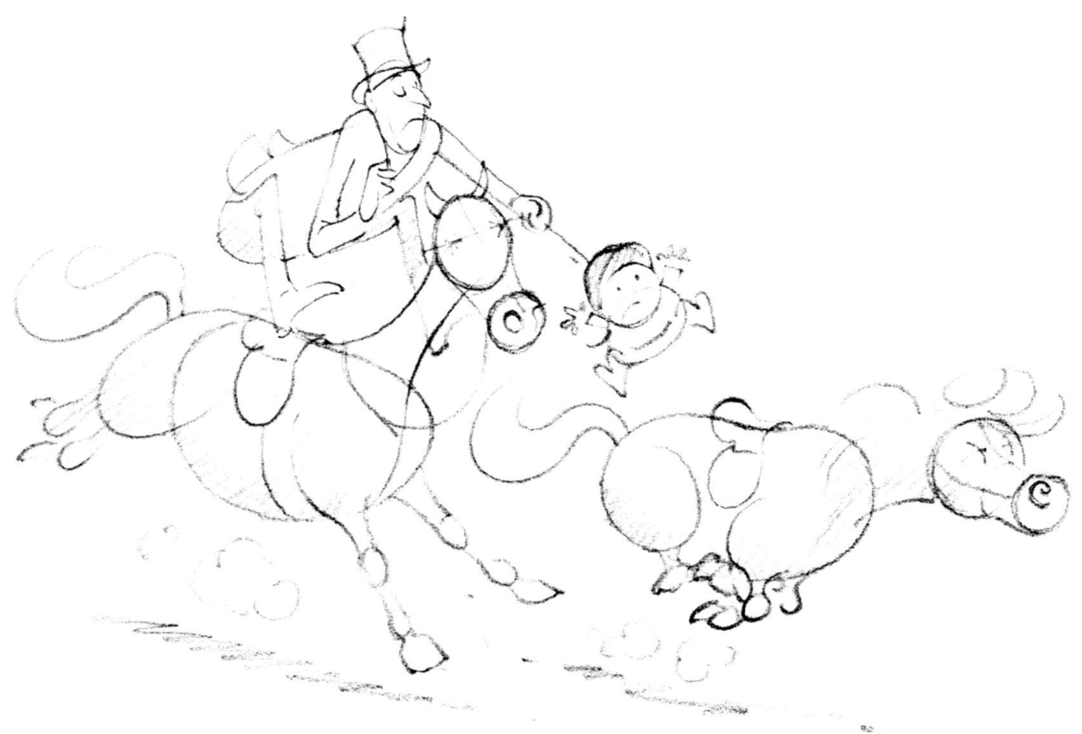

Stage II

Now we must make a full-size drawing of the composition chosen, but before we do so we must think about possible changes if these will improve the design. We must think about movement and balance and change anything which was not quite satisfactory in the first sketch.

The legs of both animals made much the same sort of pattern, so we have changed the legs of the pony to add contrast and variety and also because the pony now gives us another stage of the galloping movement (exaggerated, of course) and adds to the feeling of progressive movement. Both riders wore the same kind of hat. Changing one of them adds variety of shapes. The direction of light and main tones should be considered at this stage.

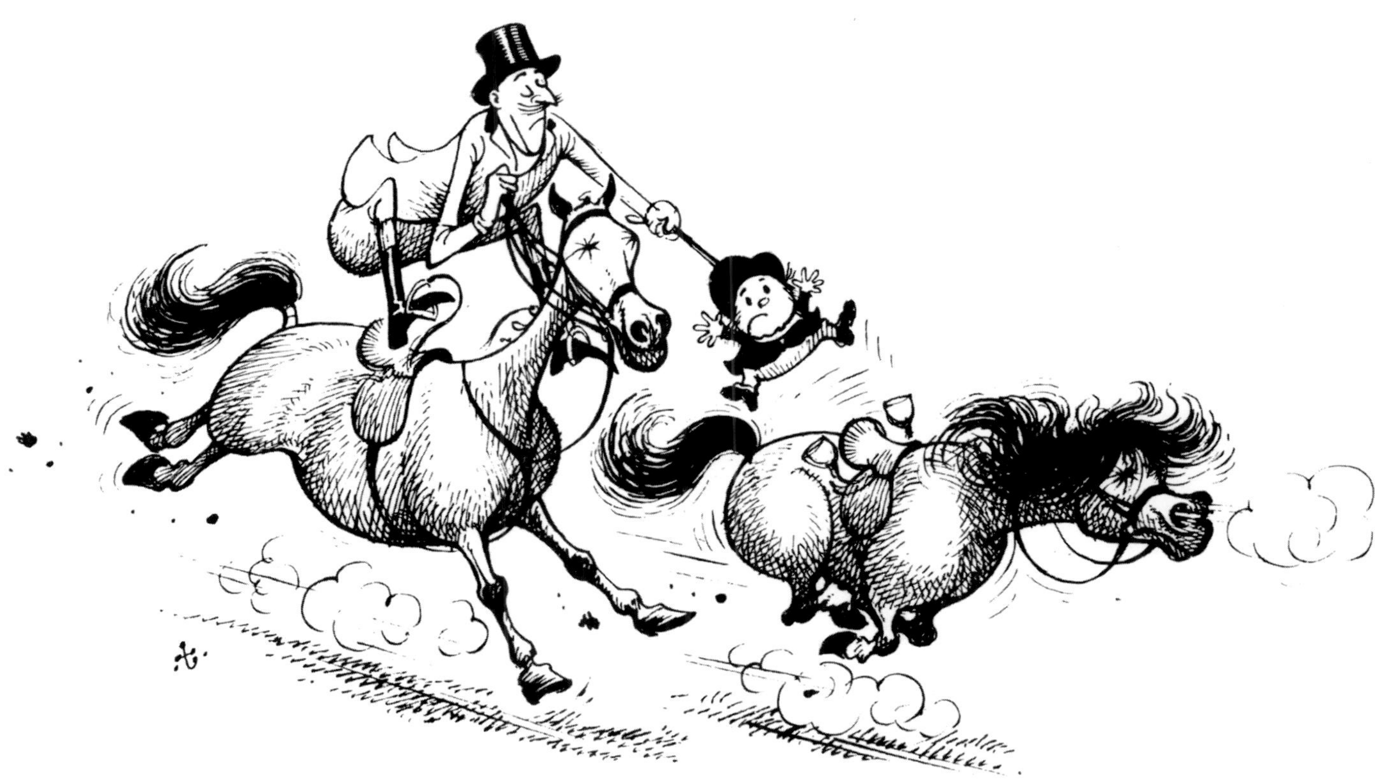

Stage III

Some artists like to trace their preparatory drawing off on to a clean sheet of paper before doing the finished work. I find it less tedious to redraw it if necessary, but this is a purely personal matter.

The important thing is to enjoy working on the finished drawing; have fun with it, or it may look tired and overworked.

The object should be to make it look as fresh and spontaneous as possible, however much toil and effort may have gone into its creation.

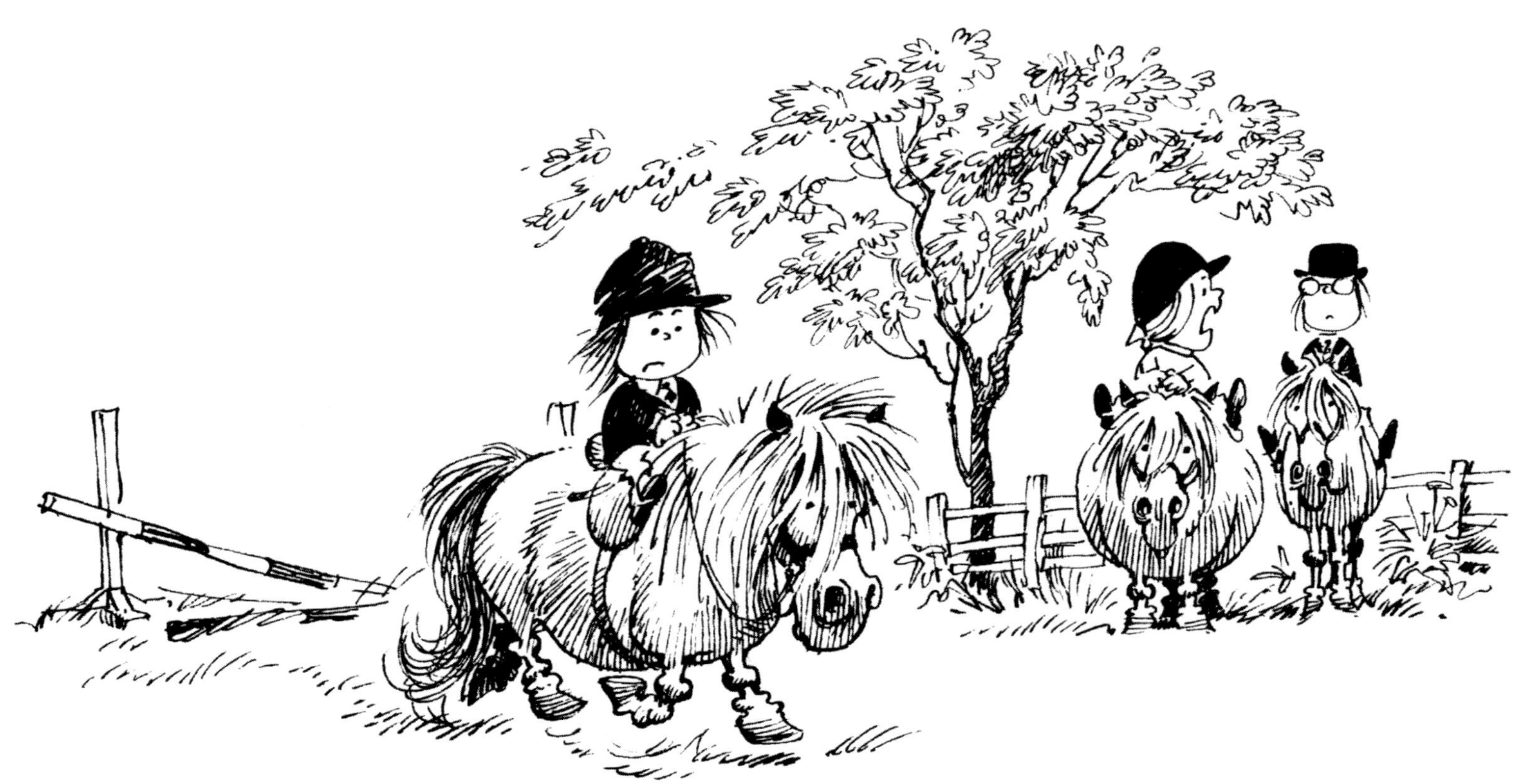

'She seemed to lose all ambition when Mark Phillips got married.'

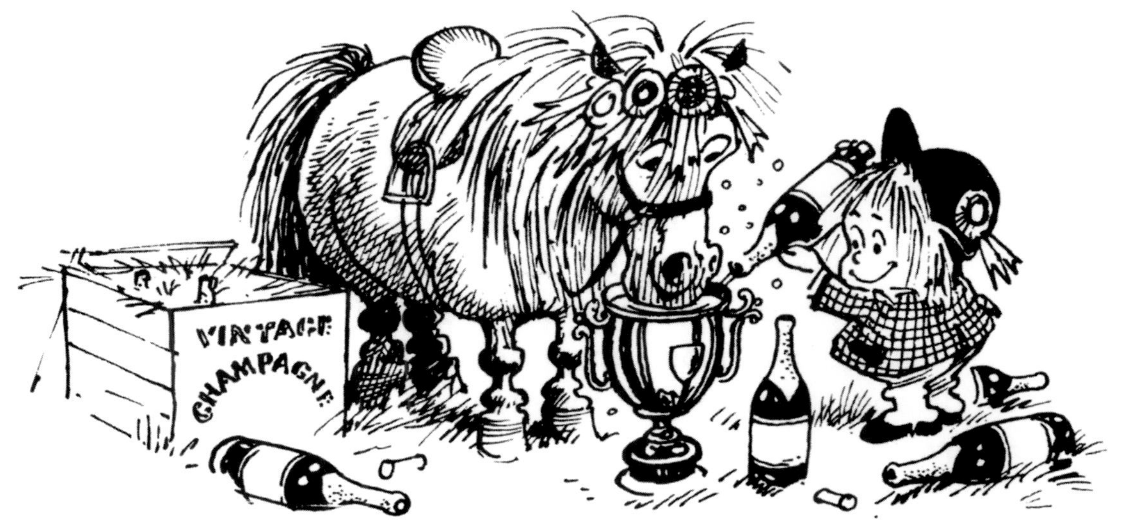

Summing up

This has been a little book about drawing ponies; in fact it has been concerned mainly with how I go about drawing them.

However, on reflection I am sure that in many ways it would have been very similar if I had been asked to write about drawing cows or pigs or monkeys. The main principles of drawing apply whatever subject one happens to be concerned with.

The fact of the matter is that there are no rules in the strict sense of the word for producing a picture. It is unlikely that the prehistoric hunters who painted on the walls of their caves worried over much about rules, yet their pictures have an effect as satisfying and delightful in their own way as anything which has been done since.

The thing that matters ultimately is the drawing, rather than the methods used to achieve it, and no two people will go about it in exactly the same way, which is why pictures and picture making is so endlessly fascinating.

There are, however, certain principles which are helpful in putting young artists on the right lines, and I make no apology for repeating some of them.

Knowledge is never wasted, and the more we can know about a subject the better. Those cavemen may not have cared much about rules, but there is no doubt whatever that they knew the subjects they painted very well indeed.

Study your subject then and use every possible means of doing so. From photographs and books and from the work of other people, but most important of all, from personal contact with the subject and by drawing from life.

Remember your sketchbook. It is the most important piece of equipment. Using it will teach you about your subject and teach you about drawing.

It is pointless to try to do with pen or pencil what a camera can do much better, but this is no excuse for lazy, inaccurate drawing. However inventive and fertile your imagination may be, your pictures will be better if based on careful observation and careful draughtsmanship.

Learn from the work of other artists by all means, but do not try to produce the same pictures. At best you can only be a clever mimic. Your own personal interpretation of a subject is the only one which will have any real meaning and life of its own.

Experiment with materials. Again, there are no rules unless you are working for publication in a certain paper. What will excite one person may bore another. The very nature of materials will suggest new fields of interest and exploration. Materials for drawing and painting are infinite in their variety nowadays, and it is well worth trying anything you can afford.

Remember, however, that the most delightful results are often achieved with the most restricted materials, and that the limits set by a given material may often add enormously to the visual pleasure of a piece of work.

Drawing is hard work but it is also absorbing and delightful work. Whatever you are working on, enjoy it. Your delight will show in your finished work, and those who see it will share your pleasure.

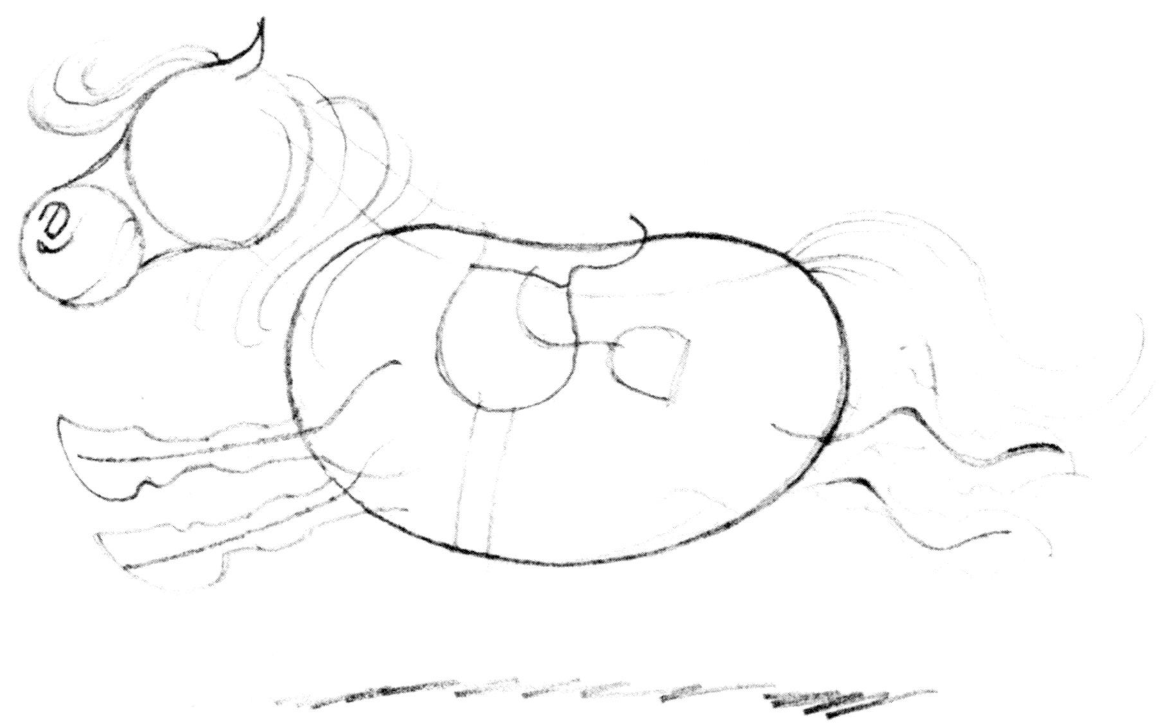

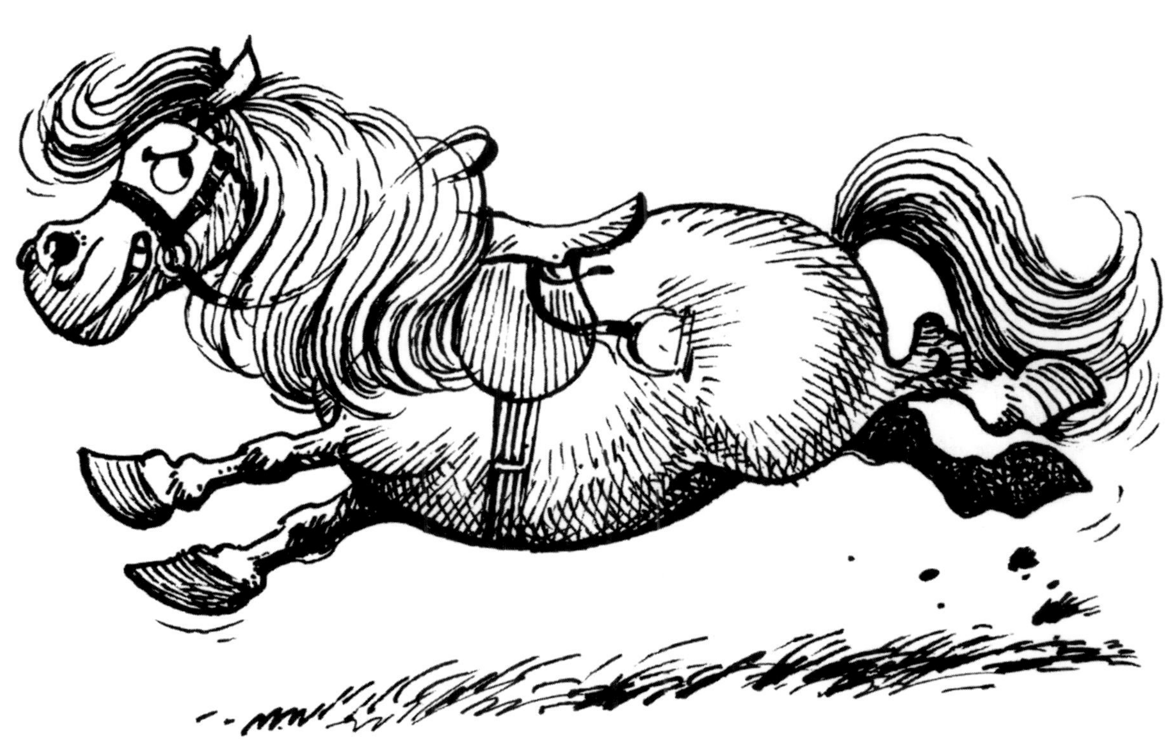